IRAN's

DEMOCRATIC REVOLUTION

IRAN's
DEMOCRATIC REVOLUTION

The International Committee in Search of Justice (ISJ)

Iran's Democratic Revolution

First published in January 2023

The International Committee in Search of Justice (ISJ)

ISBN-10: 94-6475-220-3 (Paperback)

ISBN-13: 978-9-4647522-0-5 (Paperback)

ISBN-10: 94-6475-222-X (eBook)

ISBN-13: 978-9-4647522-2-9 (eBook)

Printed by The International Committee in Search of Justice (ISJ)

https://www.isjcommittee.com/

This book is dedicated to those who sacrificed for a free and democratic future for the Iranian people, especially Iranian women.

ACKNOWLEDGMENTS

The world will be a better place when Iran is free and its people living under a democratic republic in peace with its neighbors and the world. The Iranian people have shown us that the path to this ideal is necessarily through the popular abolishment of the present evil regime and the least we can do is to stand with them and remove the impediments that appeasement policy in the West has created towards this goal over the past few decades.

My first acknowledgment is to the courageous women and youth of Iran who have stood up so bravely to throw off the shackles of the religious fascism ruling their country. They have sacrificed much and have inspired the world.

I would also like to acknowledge the inspiring role of Mrs. Maryam Rajavi and the NCRI and MEK for their tireless efforts and enormous sacrifice in organizing resistance to this regime inside and outside Iran, and for creating a democratic vision and plan for future Iran.

As Senator Joseph Lieberman said on December 8, 2022 "The lights that NCRI, MEK, and organizations of Iranian American communities have been lighting for decades, are now being held high. They have been spread by millions of Iranians. What is true is that the torches that the NCRI held up for years and have now been lighting the candles throughout the country, have not diminished at all. The torch of the NCRI and the MEK grows brighter in my opinion, with each passing day. The organization gives us confidence that the current regime will be overthrown, and most importantly, that when it is there, there will be leaders ready to guide Iran smoothly into its free and democratic future."

Finally, I would like to thank the insightful interpretation and analysis of the various aspects of this momentous sea change in Iran by the authors in this anthology. If it were not for their brilliant and tireless efforts and their prescient understanding of events unfolding in Iran, this book would not exist.

Alejo Vidal Quadras

President

International Committee in Search of Justice (ISJ)

Barcelona, December 2022

CONTENTS

FOREWORD

Women's rights are human rights. This is an obvious and indeed a U.N. recognized principle. The progress of women's rights in any country is the benchmark for the status of respect for human rights in every country. This is even more true about Iran. In no country have women been so systematically and extensively discriminated against and suppressed, both in law and practice, for such a long time. In no country have women been engaged in a political struggle to the extent that Iranian women have. In no country since the beginning of the 20th century have there been so many female political prisoners executed. Indeed, the religious dictatorship in Iran has arrested tens of thousands of women, inflicted the most horrific torture upon them and executed thousands. Mahsa Amini was murdered for not wearing the veil "properly".

It is this backdrop of misogyny that explains the bravery and leadership of women in the current uprising against the regime.

Young girls stand up against the forces of repression with unparalleled courage and shout "death to the dictator." At first, it was thought that Iranian women were simply opposing mandatory veiling. The regime tried to promote this line to gloss over the depth of the movement's demands. However, Iranian history shows that Iranian women have been at the forefront of the struggle for democracy in their country. My own conversations with Iranian women over many years also bear this out.

Of course, there is no doubt that the protestors are opposed to mandatory hijab. The right to freely choose their attire is one of the basic demands of Iranian women but — as all their other fundamental rights— it can only be met in a democratic society and not under a fundamentalist theocratic regime. We have seen Iranian women with and without hijab standing together in fighting for human rights in Iran. They are all for freedom.

The hopes and dreams of these women are much deeper than the issue of the veil, as the scale of the resistance demonstrates. They seek full gender equality and a democratic government in Iran. They know that this dream can only be achieved by overthrowing the regime and establishing the separation of religion and state. One of the current slogans that women and men are shouting on the streets of Teheran these days is very telling: "With or without hijab, we march towards revolution."

There is an iconic figure that represents the fight of Iranians against the mullahs ruling Iran, who I have come to know over the years. Maryam Rajavi is the President-elect of the National Council of Resistance of Iran (NCRI). As a Muslim woman, Mrs. Rajavi practices gender equality in all aspects, including political leadership. Years ago, she told me that women were the force for change in Iran, and that the mullahs, who underestimate them, would take the final blow from them. Mrs. Rajavi has been a staunch defender of women who choose not to wear the hijab, as much as of those who do. Her motto has consistently been: "No to mandatory hijab, No to mandatory religion, No to any mandatory regime."

Iranian politics is extremely complex. Forty-three years ago, the people of Iran overthrew the Shah's dictatorship to establish freedom and democracy. But religious fundamentalists, led by Khomeini, hijacked this popular revolution, and hastily imposed another dictatorship, this one of a religious nature.

Now, the chant is, "Down with the oppressor, be it the Shah or the Supreme Leader." The apparently odd reference to the Shah is explicable by reference to the historical alliance between the monarchy and clergy. During the 1953 coup against Prime Minister Mohammad Mosaddegh, a liberal reformist who was opening a democratic path for Iranians, the religious leader at the time, Ayatollah Kashani, formed an alliance with the Shah to bring Mosaddegh down, accusing him of being a "Communist." That unholy alliance between the Shah and the mullahs brought a sad end to an Iranian spring that was about to flourish decades ago. Today, the mullahs are in power. But the monarchists, despite all their enmity against this regime, prefer this religious tyranny to the free and democratic republic that the Iranian people in the streets are demanding.

During the years in which I became more acquainted with the Iranian Resistance, I was exposed to various accusations against the main opposition, the Mujahedin-e Khalq (MEK). It took me some time to realize that the Iranian regime was and is carrying out a massive misinformation campaign against this organization, specifically targeting Maryam Rajavi, the NCRI's President-elect. Among the detractors are supposedly independent journalists and self-styled human rights activists. Two things made the falsehoods clear to me. First, I read and studied as much as possible about the Iranian Resistance and about the denunciations made against them. It took me sometime to realize that I was faced with a sophisticated disinformation campaign, where true elements, such as the presence of the organization in Iraq in the last two years of the Iran-Iraq war, were distorted. Finally, I concluded that the origin of these accusations could always be traced directly to the Iranian regime. Second, after getting to know Maryam Rajavi and after many conversations with many members and supporters of the Iranian Resistance, it became clear to me that there were no grounds to portray them as terrorists. Given my background, I have developed an expertise in identifying such actors.

There was for me no doubt that these Iranian women and men were real democrats who have gone beyond the call of duty to free their country. As if to prove me right, I was targeted, amongst other public figures, during a Free Iran rally at Villepinte near Paris, by terrorists in June 2018. The Belgian judiciary sentenced these terrorists to 20 years in prison. They were Iranian diplomats and spies recruited by the mullah's regime.

What is happening in Iran today is undoubtedly a revolution. After four months of bloody repression, the killing of hundreds of people, and the imprisonment and torture of tens of thousands of detainees, the regime has not been able to silence the people's uprising. The undeniable fact is that there will be no return to the status quo before the murder of Mahsa Amini that ignited these protests.

Today's nationwide uprising of the Iranian people is not an overnight phenomenon. It has roots in 43 years of resistance. Similarly, the leading role of women is not a transient phenomenon.

It emerged from the long struggle by Iranian women against the misogynist regime of the mullahs.

In my opinion, Senator Lieberman was correct in his remarks at the conference entitled "The Iranian people's uprising for a secular, non-nuclear republic" at the US Senate on December 8, 2022: "And let me say first that as we consider what should happen now, we have a historic and moral responsibility to look back and to pay tribute to all those who have held this hope of a free Iran alive for decades. They are courageous Iranian patriots both inside and outside the country, and I will say in this regard that no organization has done more to light Candles of hope and freedom through some of the darkest days of repression and mass murder in Iran than the National Council of Resistance of Iran led by Mrs. Maryam Rajavi and really history must note that. But we can do it by noting it and expressing our appreciation itself."

In such a situation, the international community should go beyond expressing statements of condemnation of the regime by expressing sympathy with the Iranian people. It should take practical and concrete measures. It is time to use the snapback mechanism to revive the resolutions of the United Nations Security Council. It is time to recognize the right of the Iranian people to defend themselves against the cruelty of the mullahs. Regime embassies should be closed in Europe. Let's not forget that in June 2018, one of the regime's "diplomats" in Europe tried to blow up the annual meeting of the National Council of Resistance in Paris, where hundreds of political figures from all over the world were present, in addition to nearly a hundred thousand other participants. It is time for a new Iran policy in America and Europe. A policy that focuses on ending the culture of impunity for the regime and begin to hold the leaders of this regime to account for genocide and four decades of crimes against humanity."

Ingrid Betancourt

Former Colombian Presidential Candidate and Senator

Paris, France, December 2022

PREFACE

Iran has been going through successive revolutions since the Constitutional Revolution of the early 1900s that culminated in its first elected parliament and limited the monarchy's absolute power. However, foreign interference and successive coups robbed Iranians of the chance to establish a democratic legacy: The democratic government of Mohammad Mosaddegh in the 1950s was short-lived.

The ouster of the nationalist Prime Minister Mosaddegh by a CIA/MI6 engineered coup in 1953 left Iran in the hands of a detested dictator, who in his later years became megalomaniacal, despotic, and who suppressed democratic forces with torture and execution.[1] The violence that the Shah's regime unleashed against Iranian society was the least of the damage he did. The political vacuum he created for Ruhollah Khomeini became his lasting legacy.

The Khomeini regime, from which Ali Khamenei and his cohorts hail, is the most recent reincarnation of authoritarianism and despotism in Iran. The regime rode a wave of "anti-imperialist" victimhood, subdued Iranian society with foreign wars and crises, and held a guilt-ridden Western community at bay with ethno-religious claims to alternative theories of "Islamic" human rights, "Islamic" democracy, and "Islamic" justice.

The new Iranian revolution unfolding before our eyes, pursuing the goals of freedom and democracy of the 1979 revolution, refutes those claims, tears down the regime's lies, and lays claim to Iranian society's inalienable and universal right to individual and civil liberties, a democratic republic, and the rule of law.

---

[1] Cochran, Alexander, Ridgeway, James and Albert, Jan. 1977. "Beautiful Butchers: The Shah Serves Up Caviar and Torture - The Village Voice." Village Voice. November 14, 1977. https://www.villagevoice.com/2022/11/15/beautiful-butchers-the-shah-serves-up-caviar-and-torture/.

This anthology of writings, by expert analysts with insights into the complicated political landscape of Iran, deals with the recent uprising sparked by the murder in custody of the innocent 23-year-old Iranian woman, Mahsa Amini on September 16, 2022. Ever since 2017, and throughout 2018 and 2019, when uprisings rocked Iran with increased frequency and cataclysmic force, observers and social scientists began warning that the regime would face society's fury in the next social upheaval around the corner.

The uprising was therefore not unforeseen, nor can it be understood in the limited context, however tragic, of one unjust and extrajudicial killing. The criminal killing of Mahsa Amini was not a one-off injustice, but a byproduct of an illegitimate system of government that the people have shown they will no longer tolerate. These are not just single-issue protests, but a broad and geographically expansive movement to dethrone Ali Khamenei and his clerical dictatorship. The uprising is ultimately the product of decades of pent-up frustration and fury at a regime that is yet another embodiment of past despotic systems. It is also rooted in over four decades of relentless resistance and sacrifice, which includes tens of thousands of martyrs and many more who endured years of imprisonment and the most severe torture.

In this anthology, the authors lend insight and clarity to puzzling aspects of a complex movement. In the first essay, Dr. Behrouz Pouyan, an assistant university professor and a political analyst in Tehran, writing under his pseudonym for security reasons, guides the reader through the current uprising and its distinctive features.

Ambassador J. Kenneth Blackwell, an author and senior fellow for human rights and constitutional governance at the Family Research Council, and a visiting professor at the Liberty University School of Law, dissects and lays bare the regime's repression during the current round of protests.

Professor Ivan Sascha Sheehan, from the University of Baltimore's Public and International Affairs Department, discusses the issue of unity among opposition forces, touching upon those that ousted the

Shah in 1979, and delving into the basis for unity and what it means to be united.

Alejo Vidal-Quadras, a former First Vice President of the European Parliament and President of the International Committee in Search of Justice, presents the political alternative to the falling regime of the mullahs in Iran.

Struan Stevenson, former member of EU Parliament and Coordinator of the Campaign for Iran Change, exposes the regime's tactics of coercion, terrorism, disinformation, and political manipulation, especially its demonization campaigns directed against its nemesis, the MEK.

Robert Torricelli, former US Senator from New Jersey, discusses the international community's role in the new Iranian revolution and contributes policy recommendations.

Uprising: The Features

By Dr. Behrouz Pouyan, Tehran, Iran

The Spark

On September 13, 2022, Mahsa (Jina) Amini, a 22-year-old woman from Saqqez, Kurdistan province, who had travelled to Tehran along with her family, was detained on charges of "mal-veiling" by a branch of the regime's security forces tasked with suppressing women, particularly in relation to their attire. She was transferred to a police station to obtain her commitment to the regime's misogynist laws. While in custody, Mahsa was beaten severely by agents of the State Security Forces (SSF), and later died in hospital because of skull fractures.

Following this tragedy, not the first instance of such state killings carried out with impunity, massive waves of anti-regime protests broke out in Iran starting on September 16, 2022, initially in condemnation of Mahsa's murder. By December the uprising had spread to at least 300 cities in all 31 provinces of the country, including many universities and high schools. On some days during this period, at least 60 locations in Tehran alone flared with protests. With the uprising in its fourth month, more than 700 protesters have been killed. Over 70 of those killed were under 18 years of age, including a 10-year-old boy, Kian Pirfalak, in Izeh city in southwest Khuzestan province, and an eight-year-old girl, Mona Naqib, in Zahedan. To date, 601 slain protesters have been identified by the main opposition Mujahedin-e Khalq (MEK). In addition, over four months of protests in Iran, hundreds have been wounded and more than 30,000 have been detained. Some of the detainees have been sentenced to death on the outrageous charge of *"Moharebeh"* (waging war on God). Two executions have been carried out already resulting in the death of Mohsen Shekari in Tehran and

Majid Reza Rahnavard in Mashhad on December 8 and 12, respectively.

The uprising formed in protest to the regime's killing of Mahsa Amini in an unplanned and somewhat spontaneous way. But it owes its continuation, expansion, and longevity to the presence of an organized resistance across Iran. A resistance with deep social and political roots in fighting the suppression of popular demands for the past 40 years by the mullahs' rule. Thus, the killing of Mahsa acted as a spark that exploded the powder keg of Iranian society. This explosive state has its roots in extensive socio-political suppression, egregious violation of citizens' human rights, economic ruin, high commodity prices, poverty, unemployment, hunger, and environmental disasters emanating from corruption and mismanagement, among many other factors.

Expansive Scope

The recent uprisings cut across social and economic divides in the country, with virtually all social classes united in the call for regime overthrow. Demonstrating its reach and depth, universities and high schools, bazaar merchants, workers, athletes, artists, performers, ethnic minorities, lower and middle classes, and large portions of the upper classes as well have joined the nationwide movement.

The movement is revolutionary in that it does not seek illusory "reforms" but the full dismantlement of the regime. Students in middle schools, high schools, and universities are involved in these protests in one way or another, and the general populace also advance this revolutionary uprising through day and night protests in various cities and towns, starting fires on the streets, confronting suppressive forces, chanting anti-regime slogans from rooftops at nights, drivers honking their horns in support of protesters on the streets, and people taking in the injured to their homes and giving refuge to protesters or activists being pursued by security forces. University students have spearheaded the defiance that has shocked the regime, appearing in demonstrations and strikes at campuses day after day, despite brutal beatings, arrests, and attacks. High school students have joined in as well by chanting anti-regime slogans on the streets after exiting their schools. The overwhelming majority of Iranians reject the theocratic dictatorship and support the uprising.

Since this uprising has deep historical roots and emerges based on the people's fundamental demands that have been suppressed during the mullahs' rule, from the beginning of the protests, protesters formulated slogans that were against the entirety of the regime, and which had a revolutionary character. Demonstrators in neighborhoods of various cities represent a variety of social sectors and economic classes. They are in the streets to create fundamental and structural political changes, specifically calling for the overthrow of the clerical regime. Workers, farmers, teachers, doctors, nurses, bazaar merchants, and other social sectors and groups, and social groupings who in the past might have been characterized as forming the mullahs' social base, have all lined up against the regime in today's revolutionary circumstances.

Students and Iran's new generation, women at the forefront, are providing the impetus for the movement. The pent-up anger over decades of suppression, corruption and plunder is now erupting with fervor. A modern, vibrant, and technologically savvy generation of youth poses an existential challenge to the medieval theocracy's rule. This is a generation that most strikingly does not have the slightest affinity with the ruling mullahs or their policies.

The persistence and increased organization of the uprisings demonstrate that they are not spontaneous or leaderless. Mujahedin-e Khalq (MEK) Resistance Units play a pivotal role in guiding and organizing the uprisings. One demand, that of overthrow of the regime as expressed by participants in the uprising in their slogan of "Death to Khamenei," has dominated the uprising's spirit since the outset.

State-affiliated reports published in the regime's media show that much of the population suffers from serious economic hardships.

Unemployment, poverty, price hikes and unbridled inflation, lack of access to healthcare, and environmental crises have become commonplace and omnipresent. Evermore astonishing that short-term economic demands are not voiced in recent protests. Rather, the slogans have revolved around the imperative of overthrowing the regime in its entirety. This is because over the past 40 years, various sectors of the Iranian population have learned and concluded that myriad problems and crises will be solved only when the political economy, the regime, is removed and a democratic republic is established in its place.

Another important characteristic of the uprising is a reiteration of Iranians' rejection of the monarchy. The Iranian people are keenly aware that a return to past dictatorships is not an option. They are looking to the future. One of the main chants in this regard is "Death to the oppressor, be it the Shah or the Supreme Leader." Young Iranians, women, and the broader population have clearly and explicitly expressed their desire for a secular and democratic republic that rejects both the current ruling theocracy and the previous monarchy.

Women and Youth in the Lead

Iran's youth and women who have borne the brunt of the regime's repression, have made it clear in these uprisings that they seek nothing less than the downfall of the religious dictatorial regime that has ruined their lives, their future, and their country. For example, a 17-year-old female protester in a central Iranian city, who is representative of those out on the streets challenging the regime's security forces, told Reuters, "Hey world, hear me: I want a revolution. I want to live freely, and I am ready to die for it. Instead of dying every minute under this regime's repression, I prefer to die with their (security forces) bullets in protests for freedom".[1]

---

[1] 2022. "Iran toughens crackdown as some oil workers reported to join protests." Reuters. October 11, 2022. https://www.reuters.com/world/middle-east/iran-intensifies-crackdown-kurdish-cities-unrest-persists-2022-10-10/.

For Iran observers, women's extraordinary leadership in demanding the regime's downfall is hardly shocking. Misogyny is coded into the theocracy's DNA, so women have borne the brunt of the mullahs' oppression. The anger over decades of suppression, corruption, and plunder is erupting.

Countless threats, intimidation, and misogynist aggression have failed to deter women. For the most part, this is because 35 years of women's leadership in the organized Resistance[2] against the regime has inspired Iran's women, who are not just fighting for their own rights, but rather to free their nation.

The world has been witnessing the courage, commitment, and wisdom of Iranian women confronting a regime that considers them as second-class citizens. The courage emanates from knowing your foe in the misogynist Islamic fundamentalism ideology, which started mandatory hijab for women as its first repressive initiative only weeks after it took power in 1979. And by looking at women of the resistance who for decades played an increasingly significant role in the nationwide struggle against the regime. Iranian women know that none of their rights will ever be recognized so long as this regime is in power, and women's freedom can only be secured in a free and democratic Iran.

The root of this bravery is in the determination of thousands of women who stood firm against the regime for many long years, particularly during the 2000s. They refused to give in or submit to the regime at the cost of their lives. A cursory look at the history of Iran's organized resistance reveals a long list of female activists, who laid the foundations for today's defiant female generation as they stand up to the vicious mullahs' regime.

During the 1988 massacre of some 30,000 political prisoners, thousands of women prisoners chose to say "no" to Khomeini and the mullahs' demands to renounce their activism and organizational

---

[2] Rajavi, Maryam. 2010. "Women, A Force for Change".

affiliation. Based on reports by those who survived, in many prisons, entire populations of MEK female prisoners were executed.

Twenty-seven years ago, Mrs. Maryam Rajavi, the President-elect of the National Council of Resistance of Iran (NCRI), delivered a speech entitled "Women: Voice of the Oppressed," to 25,000 Iranians gathered at London's Earls Court, in which she underscored the circumstances and role of women in Iran. She addressed the ruling mullahs and said: "You have used all possible forms of humiliation, oppression, repression, torture, and murder against Iranian women. But be certain that you will receive the fatal blow from those you never even considered. Of course, your reactionary nature does not allow you to consider them. But rest assured your oppressive rule will be swept away by Iran's conscious and free women." [3]

Unyielding

The initial trigger for the uprising was the murder of Mahsa Amini and the general expression of public disgust by the Iranian people towards the regime's oppression of women. But due to the inflamed and explosive situation of society, the uprising has gone much further and as declared in their slogans, it has evolved to target the "principle of the system," meaning the entire regime and everything for which it stands.

In testament to the radical nature of the uprising, people have demonstrably lost their fear of the theocracy. The regime has tried to marshal its brutal Basij militia and IRGC forces and deployed its signature ruthless suppression. It has massively disrupted the Internet to carry out its criminal repression in total blackout. But as shown by the extraordinary persistence and revolutionary nature of the nationwide uprising, the suppressive forces have proven largely ineffective in crushing the ongoing revolution.

---

[3] Rajavi, Maryam. 1996. "Iran: Women are Force for Change - Maryam Rajavi." Maryam-rajavi.com. June 21, 1996. https://www.maryam-rajavi.com/en/iran-women-are-force-for-change/.

The wall of repression is showing visible cracks, and fear of the regime has been replaced with outrage and a determination to bring about revolutionary change, as can be seen in protesters fighting back against suppressive forces. In dozens of cases, people arrested by the security forces or plainclothes thugs (Basij militias affiliated with the IRGC or the Ministry of Intelligence) have been set free through counterattacks against those forces. Several Basij members have been killed during clashes with protesters whom they had ruthlessly attacked. Revolutionary activists have announced loud and clear that "We do not fear anymore; we fight." The regime has admitted to at least 103 deaths and more than 3,000 injuries among its security forces. Many IRGC and Basij centers have been torched, police stations taken over, and offices of Khamenei's representatives in various cities attacked, as the practice has gone mainstream.

"Death to Khamenei"

The revolutionary nature of the nationwide uprising in Iran is best illustrated through its slogans. Social media is abuzz with numerous videos appearing daily, showing demonstrators chanting slogans like "Death to Dictator;" "Death to Khamenei;" "Death to the Oppressor, be it the Shah or the Leader;" and "This year is the year of sacrifice, Seyyed Ali [Khamenei] will be overthrown".[4] Furthermore, these slogans are not confined to particular cities, and are chanted across Iran by almost all demographics.

The revolutionary activists communicate with each other, the public and the enemy in the language of slogans. The unifying slogan has been the rejection of Khamenei and his regime with slogans of death to dictator and death to Khamenei. At this stage, the affirmative slogan has been the "Freedom, freedom, freedom" slogan. The people realize that Khamenei represents the regime as a whole and are targeting him fearlessly and directly as they pursue regime

---

[4] Serjoie, Kay Armin. 2022. "Protests in Iran Have Shaken the Islamic Republic." Time. September 24, 2022. https://time.com/6216024/iran-protests-islamic-republic-response/.

change. The IRGC and the Basij, as well as the State Security Forces, are all tools to keep the regime in power.

Some other slogans chanted in various cities during the protests include: "We will fight, we will die, we will take back our Iran," "We swear to our fallen heroes, we will persevere until the end," "Canons, tanks, machine guns are no longer effective; tell my mother she no longer has a daughter," "This is the year of sacrifice, Khamenei is going to be overthrown," "From Kurdistan to Tehran, my life is for Iran," and "From Zahedan to Tehran, my life is for Iran."

Unified for Regime Change

Iran is a country that is blessed with having different ethnic and religious affiliations. Kurds, Baluchis, and Arabs, among others, have their own ethnic characteristics, and over the years, they have suffered double oppression under the regimes of the Shah and the mullahs. They have always rightfully sought their rights to learn and speak their own language, wear their own attire, and practice their own religion, which is predominantly Sunni Islam. Despite the regime's utmost efforts to paint the Kurds and Baluchis as separatists, the common slogan of Iranians in Tehran, Azerbaijan, Kurdistan, or Zahedan has been: "From Zahedan to Kurdistan to Tehran, my life for Iran." This slogan has clearly neutralized the mullahs' plots, demonstrating that those who form Iran's ethnic mosaic are all united in their opposition to this regime. The National Council of Resistance of Iran announced its plan for the autonomy of Kurdistan, and its plan for separation of religion and state in the 1980s to combat the regime's oppression of Iran's minorities.

Although ethnic and religious demands based on a history of minority suppression exist, all ethnic and religious affiliations in Iran today, in the context of the larger struggle for freedom and the overthrow of the religious dictatorship, consciously prioritize the main national demand. Everyone knows that the realization of their own rights can only be achieved with the overthrow of the current ruling system and establishment of a democratic republic. By this demand, the Iranian people have not only rejected religious tyranny, but also the former monarchical dictatorship, which paved the way for the mullahs' rule by suppressing democratic forces. In their eyes, in tomorrow's Iran and in the context of a democratic republic, all Iranian citizens will have equal rights, and those who were doubly oppressed must be compensated.

Popularly Organized

The Iranian people realize that deep-seated and multi-dimensional misery in Iran is a byproduct of the ruling regime, and this awareness motivates shattering calls for total regime change. The expansion, longevity, radical political messaging against the regime, and uniformity of slogans are all indicative of the uprising's organization. This increased organization leaves little room for plots hatched by the regime and its international allies to derail the movement, ensuring its staying power.

The regime was aware of the explosive state of society and the possibility of another uprising. Khamenei's engineering of the sham presidential election and the purging of all rival candidates to ensure that Ebrahim Raisi was installed, despite a nationwide boycott, was meant to thwart another uprising. But despite these moves, Iran has witnessed an unprecedented eruption of rage over the past four months. Sustaining the nationwide uprising without a significant level of organization and coordination would have been impossible.

Regime officials and state-run media continue to express anxiety over the protests' organized nature. The IRGC-run Fars news agency wrote: "Today, the country is suffering from the conspiracies of the MEK, and they are trying to create insecurity in the society with various lies, ranging from the murder of Mahsa Amini to the killing of people and students by the police. In the meantime, people from different backgrounds have fueled this fire and by republishing falsehoods and lies, they have caused chaos in society and destroyed the lives and property of ordinary people and are also damaging public property." Hosseinali Haji-Deligani, a member of the parliament's presidium, said: "According to eyewitnesses, the units in recent protests were organized and tasked with destruction. They used new tactics to fight [security] forces, confirming they had been trained." [5] In an interview with the state-run Tasnim news agency, Hassan Rezania, the political and security deputy of Hamedan Governorate said: "There are organized units which set some places on fire. These actions indicate that they are organized. They have attempted to take over governorates in some cities." [6]

The regime's officials are keenly aware of the impact of the MEK's Resistance Units. On October 10, the IRGC Brigadier General Mohammad Bagheri, Chief of Staff for the regime's Armed Forces, expressed the regime's utter fear of the Resistance Units. He said: "The very few scenes of chaos in some parts of the country, and the enemy's focus on the ethnic and religious minority, all indicate the enemy has waged a full-fledged war on [the regime]. In this war, the evil [MEK] ... act as the enemy's pawns." [7] The commander of the State Security Forces (SSF), Hossain Ashtari, told[8] the state-run Entekhab website: "Those who disrupt security and damage public property will be punished. We would decisively deal with them. Rioters, led by the MEK, are willing to instigate chaos."

---

[5] 2022. "MPs: Behind the scenes of all the recent incidents and intrigues are the criminal government of Britain and the MKO." Entekhab. September 21, 2022. https://www.entekhab.ir/fa/news/ 695889/نماینده-مجلس-پشت-صحنه-همه-حوادث-ها-دولت-جنایتکار-انگلیس-و-منافقین-هستندC8%80%E2%اخیر-و-فتنه

[6] 2022. "The current of hypocrisy in the recent turmoil had entered Hamedan." Tasnim News Agency. September 24, 2022. https://www.tasnimnews.com/fa/news/1401/07/02/ 2778517/-در-نفاق-جریان اغتشاشات-اخیر-وارد-همدان-شده-بود.

[7] 2022. "Maj. Gen. Bagheri: The enemy has waged a war of parties against the Iranian people / In this war, royalist scum, the MKO and terrorist groups are the enemy's operatives." Entekhab. October 11, 2022. https://www.entekhab.ir/fa/news/ 698298.

[8] 2022. "The Commander-in-Chief of the Police Force: Arresting the rioters is not solely the responsibility of the country's police, and other agencies are also responsible for this." Entekhab. October 11, 2022. https://www.entekhab.ir/fa/news/698460.

Further to this logic, a network of organized Resistance Units affiliated with the Mujahedin-e Khalq (MEK) has been on the ground to consistently organize, guide, and direct the uprising and provide a mainstay of political guidance and stability for the movement. These units have gradually increased in number, size, geographic expanse, and operational capabilities. In the past, they played a key role during the 2017 and 2019 uprisings. The regime's top leaders, as well as various senior and lower-ranking officials, constantly express alarm, and anxiety over the growing role of Resistance Units inside Iran.

In a bid to discourage university students to join the ranks of the resistance units, the regime's president Ebrahim Raisi said in a speech to a group of Sharif University officials on October 6, 2022: "We are sure that the Sharif students will not allow ill-wishers and *Hypocrites* [MEK] to distort this university."[9] Recounting events during the current unrest, a member of the Parliament's Security Commission, Javad Karimi Qoddousi, described the protests as planned and organized, before proceeding to provide a detailed account of such activities: "In these incidents, based on what was seen, teams of five people... destroy the place. They leave quickly, and another four come from the other side."[10]

On the Cusp of Revolution

The majority of Iranians believe that the regime must be overthrown in its entirety to find solutions to the country's myriad challenges and crises. To that end, they know that the right strategy is to sustain a ceaseless attack on the mullahs' regime, particularly against its pivotal suppressive force in the IRGC.

The culture of defiance, which is manifested in the targeting and torching of all regime symbols and confronting its repressive forces with any means, has led to the continuation of the uprisings. The

---

[9] State-affiliated Farda News, October 6, 2022.
[10] Khorasan TV channel, September 29, 2022.

persistence of anti-regime demonstrations throughout the country and the fearless enthusiasm of the younger generation to confront the repressive forces, represents broader society's unified strategy of overthrowing the regime.

Demonstrators are growing more fearless and resolute. The regime's forces are stretched thin and rapidly losing morale. There are significant signs of fatigue and defections among the regime's forces. Khamenei has told the SSF commander that "your forces must not lose their morale."

In these circumstances, things will never be the same again in Iran and assuming otherwise would be extremely naive and unrealistic. The balance of power has irreversibly changed. The regime is a lot weaker, more vulnerable, and in view of even more recent killings, much more illegitimate. The Iranian people are much more determined to bring about a democratic revolution. They have gleaned important lessons from this uprising and are more empowered and prepared than ever to overthrow the regime. Change in Iran is within reach and much more accessible than it has ever been in the past four decades

Repression

By Ambassador J. Kenneth Blackwell, Cincinnati, Ohio

Even though the clerical regime has utilized its entire arsenal of suppressive forces to quell the Iranian people's uprising, the revolution is in its fourth month.

The regime was expecting another uprising, albeit not as intense. Aware of the explosive state of society, due to mounting social, economic, and political grievances, the regime anticipated another eruption, and organized its suppressive forces accordingly. Even having prepared for the inevitable, the regime was unable to prevent the uprising or to quell it.

In November 2019, because of a gasoline price hike, a major uprising occurred in Iran. The regime brutally suppressed the uprising by massacring more than 1,500 protesters and arrested and tortured tens of thousands of others. After the 2019 uprising, Ali Khamenei, the Supreme Leader of the regime, acknowledged in a speech, the organized nature of the uprising and the role of the People's Mojahedin Organization of Iran (PMOI/MEK). He knew that MEK resistance units had spread across Iran and would turn any protest into an uprising.

To prepare for future uprisings, Khamenei decided the regime should close ranks and he should consolidate the power of all three branches of government.

The Guardian Council eliminated all candidates in the presidential election, even the closest allies of Khamenei, to pave the way for the presidency of Ebrahim Raisi[1], a key member of the "Death

---

[1] "Who is Ebrahim Raisi - NCRI." Ncr-iran.org. https://www.ncr-iran.org/en/who-is-ebrahim-raisi-ncr-iran/.

Committee" which had implemented the massacre[2] of over 30,000 political prisoners, mainly supporters and members of the MEK, in the summer of 1988.

Raisi formed a government formed of officials with direct experience in violence against society, appointing fellow criminals and former IRGC commanders. For example, IRGC Brig. Gen. Mohammad Bagher Qalibaf was selected as the speaker of parliament. Mohseni Eje'i, a key official in the massacre of political prisoners in the summer of 1988, was selected as the head of the Judiciary. During the uprising, Judiciary Chief Eje'i appointed Hossein-Ali Nayeri, the head of the "Death Committee"[3] that carried out the 1988 massacre as a senior advisor.

The regime's inability to suppress the uprising, despite formidable resources and preparedness, is because of the presence of the MEK's network of resistance units in all cities of Iran and a society ready for rebellion. The MEK's resistance units lead and organize on the ground, providing energy within and demanding the world's attention without.

Repression During the 2022 Uprising

According to information provided by the MEK's network inside Iran, protests have taken place in at least 280 cities in all 31 provinces of the country, and at least 700 protesters have been killed by the end of December. The MEK has established the identities of 601 of the victims, including their names, the cities where they were killed, and the dates of their deaths. Some of the worst violence by the regime has occurred in Sistan and Baluchistan province.

---

[2] "The 1988 Massacre of 30,000 Political Prisoners in Iran - NCRI." Ncr-iran.org. https://www.ncr-iran.org/en/1988-massacre-of-political-prisoners-in-iran/.

[3] 2020. "Iran 1988 Massacre Death Commissions - NCRI." Ncr-iran.org. December 27, 2020. https://www.ncr-iran.org/en/iran-1988-massacre-of-political-prisoners/iran-1988-massacre-death-commissions/.

There are at least 60 children aged 2-17 among the victims, and the full identities of 58 of them have been obtained. Kian Pirfalak, a ten-year-old boy from Izeh, southwest Iran, was killed by security forces on November 17. He was returning home with his family when security forces opened fire on their vehicle, killing him and seriously wounding his father.

In mid-November, the regime launched an attack on Iranian Kurdish cities, particularly Mahabad and Javanrud, with IRGC armored units equipped with heavy weapons. Dozens of defenseless protesters were killed or wounded.

On September 30, 2022, Amnesty International reported that "Iran's highest military body instructed the commanders of armed forces in all provinces to "severely confront" protesters who took to the streets... The organization has documented widespread, unwarranted use of lethal force and firearms by Iranian security forces who either intended to kill protesters or should have known with a reasonable degree of certainty that their use of firearms would result in deaths." [4]

Political Detentions

At least 30,000 protesters have been detained in severe conditions in prisons and secret safe houses used by the security forces. Dozens have been killed under torture. There are numerous reports of sexual violence and rape against detained girls and boys in the prisons.

According to eyewitness reports from different parts of Iran, the regime has systematically used ambulances to transport arrested protesters. It also uses ambulances to regularly relocate security and repressive forces at protest sites. Eyewitnesses have reported

---

[4]   2022.   "Iran: Leaked documents reveal top-level orders to armed forces to 'mercilessly confront' protesters." Amnesty International. September 30, 2022. https://www.amnesty.org/en/latest/news/2022/09/iran-leaked-documents-reveal-top-level-orders-to-armed-forces-to-mercilessly-confront-protesters/.

security forces shooting at protesters from inside ambulances with no license plates.

The Iranian regime is seeking the death penalty for some detainees and has charged at least 30 people with "Moharebeh" (waging war on God), which carries the death penalty. On November 16, 2022, Amnesty International reported that "Since 13 November, the authorities have announced, in separate statements, that Revolutionary Courts in Tehran have sentenced five unnamed individuals to death for "enmity against God" (Moharebeh) and "corruption on earth" (fesad-e felarz) over what they called acts of arson, destruction of property and fatal assault against a member of the security forces during protests in Tehran province. Since 29 October, state media have regularly reported on the trial of nine men on protest-related charges carrying the death penalty. It is unclear whether the five unnamed individuals sentenced to death are among the nine men. At least 12 other people, including a woman, are also facing capital charges in connection with the protests." [5]

On October 26, 2022, U.N. human rights experts "condemned the killings and the crackdown by security forces in Iran on protesters following the death of Jina Mahsa Amini, including alleged arbitrary arrests and detentions, gender-based and sexual violence, excessive use of force, torture, and enforced disappearances. They urged that the reports be thoroughly and independently investigated and those responsible held to account." [6]

---

[5] 2022. "Iran: Chilling use of the death penalty to further brutally quell popular uprising." Amnesty International. November 16, 2022. https://www.amnesty.org/en/latest/news/2022/11/iran-chilling-use-of-the-death-penalty-to-further-brutally-quell-popular-uprising/.

[6] "Iran: Crackdown on peaceful protests since death of Jina Mahsa Amini needs independent international investigation, say UN experts." OHCHR. October 26, 2022. https://www.ohchr.org/en/press-releases/2022/10/iran-crackdown-peaceful-protests-death-jina-mahsa-amini-needs-independent.

The Regime's Lies

Mahsa Amini, a 22-year-old Kurd, was visiting Tehran when she was accosted by the "morality police" and accused of wearing her mandatory head covering too loosely. After being beaten severely at a "reeducation" center, she fell into a coma and eventually died at a hospital. Authorities' subsequent attempts to portray her death as resulting from natural causes, denied by her parents and relatives, established a pattern of disinformation that continues to the present day.

Some of the regime's claims have been absurd and sometimes self-contradictory. For example, two 16-year-old girls, Nika Shakarami and Sarina Esmailzadeh were beaten to death by security forces within the first two weeks of the unrest. Their bodies were withheld from their families to conceal evidence of abuse. Authorities later claimed that the girls committed suicide and fell from tall buildings. Official accounts shifted from accidental fall to murder at the hands of a third party other than the security forces before finally settling on "suicide."

The same lies have since been offered concerning several other young protesters, and where such claims are impossible to defend, the authorities have tended to deny responsibility by ascribing shooting deaths to "police impersonators" or "terrorists."

After the vehicle carrying 10-year-old Kian Pirfalak and his father was shot at from multiple directions on November 17 in the southwestern city of Izeh, authorities blamed "terrorists" but made no effort to account for any motives for this or the several other killings recorded on the same day and did not explain why none of the gunmen had been apprehended or killed despite the acknowledged security presence.

Pirfalak's mother was unequivocal in attributing the young boy's death to the security forces when speaking at his funeral, even saying of the authorities, "They're lying" when they refer to terrorists. "Plain-clothes forces shot my child. That is it," she said. But later that same day, she was forced to appear on state television to recant her remarks in an interview and to caution against them being "misused." This glaring contradiction by a distressed mother under duress, brought renewed attention to political detainees and the families of deceased Iranians being pressured into providing false confessions to corroborate the regime's official narratives.

Such forced confessions were also highlighted in a CNN report on November 21, [7] which focused on the authorities' use of rape as a tactic of political repression—referring to a recent detainee who had managed to speak about her experience. The report stated that "security forces brought the woman's teenage sister to the interrogation room and asked her if she was 'prepared' to let them rape her sister," after which the woman gave in and provided the confession demanded of her.

The CNN report provides several other specific examples of sexual assault in regime detention centers, for punitive as well as coercive purposes. The victims of these abuses include both women and men, some juveniles. Specific known incidents are also shockingly violent, like that of 20-year-old Armita Abbasi, who on October 17 was hospitalized after having been detained over social media posts she made openly criticizing the regime.

While plain-clothes security officers were attempting to pressure medical personnel first into saying that the rapes had occurred prior to her detention and then that Abbasi had been treated for "digestive problems", the medics themselves were exchanging private messages about the true horror of the situation. These messages leaked, causing fresh public outrage.

Yet this disrepute has done nothing to promote the resolution of Abbasi's case or any other. Rather, she remains in Fardis Prison in Karaj and is reportedly being held incommunicado, stoking concerns that she might still be experiencing equally brutal abuse,

---

[7] 2022. "Iran protests: Covert testimonies reveal sexual assaults on male and female activists as a women-led uprising spreads." Edition. November 21, 2022. https://edition.cnn.com/interactive/2022/11/middleeast/iran-protests-sexual-assault/index.html.

as the authorities work to extract false confessions and prevent her from speaking out about her mistreatment.

Tehran's strategy for managing the unrest entails isolating detainees, stealing, and hiding the bodies of those the regime has killed. There are reports of protesters' bodies being confiscated by authorities and buried secretly or released to mourners only on condition that they not hold public memorials or speak out about the true circumstances of their loved ones' deaths.

The IRGC's Role

The regime has a five-step strategy to counter the nationwide uprisings. The first is "prevention." This entails security surveillance and arrest of potential troublemakers. The second stage is "terror," meant to intimidate the public into staying off the streets by the widespread use of tear gas, water cannon, and beatings. The third stage is counterprotests or "people's involvement". The regime mobilizes repressive plainclothes and Basij paramilitary forces to put on sham counter demonstrations. The fourth stage uses nonlethal but seriously injurious weaponry, for example, bird shot and pellet guns. The fifth stage is called "the shock" stage. At this point, live ammunition is used to kill people, in some cases reaching the level of street massacres. In the city of Zahedan, the regime massacred those at Friday prayers to prevent the uprising from escalating.

A series of highly confidential intelligence reports that the NCRI has made public,[8] exposed the leading role of the Islamic Revolutionary Guard Corps (IRGC) in trying to suppress the uprising and its *modus operandi*. Some of the reports bear signatures and seals of IRGC commanders, including its Commander-in-Chief Maj. Gen. Hossein Salami.

---

[8] "NCRI Security and Counterterrorism Committee." Ncr-iran. https://www.ncr-iran.org/en/author/ncrisc/.

According to these documents, various brigades and units of the IRGC have been deployed in the crackdown, including the IRGC's Ground Forces Auxiliary HQ Brigade and the General Staff Auxiliary HQ Brigade.

The reports also show that both the threat level the regime has assigned to the protests and its perception of the role of the MEK in them are higher than what it publicly acknowledges.

In an order classified as "Urgent – Highly Confidential[9]" on October 20, the deputy commander of Sarallah HQ in Tehran (in charge of security of the capital), IRGC Brigadier Hossein Nejat, says: "Considering the increasing trend of divisionary activities by elements of the Resistance Units affiliated to the Hypocrites (pejorative term for MEK) terrorist group against classified locations, especially IRGC bases, and mindful of the directive by the Honorable Commander-in-Chief of the Islamic Revolutionary Guard Corps, ... it is necessary to identify all classified locations including military, government, and judicial locations, which are prone to divisionary actions."

According to a document classified as "highly confidential," prepared for Ali Khamenei, the regime's supreme leader, IRGC Commander-in-Chief Salami says that, in the first two weeks of the uprising, the IRGC, the State Security Forces, and the Ministry of Intelligence had detained 9,654, 9,545, and 1,246 protesters, respectively. The document adds that 42 percent of those arrested are under the age of 20. Moreover, Salami asserted that some of the detainees were "organized" members of the MEK.

These confidential reports show that there are significant levels of discontent within the IRGC's ranks. Dated October 11, 2022, a document classified as "highly confidential" and signed by Salami, outlines casualties as well as damage to the IRGC's assets, and specifically acknowledges the existence of "demoralized ...

---

[9] 2022. "Iran: IRGC Modus Operandi in Dealing With the Uprising." Ncr-iran. October 20, 2022. https://www.ncr-iran.org/en/news/iran-irgc-modus-operandi-in-dealing-with-the-uprising.

personnel". Salami orders his commanders to "refrain from deploying demoralized, disaffected and disgruntled personnel in riot control operations."

Conclusion

Despite the regime's preparedness, its violence and its disinformation, the protests continue and expand. The key role of the MEK in the uprising is revealed by this continuity and by the central role assigned to the IRGC in suppression, and in the regime's own intelligence assessments of the organized resistance.

Opposition Unity

By Ivan Sascha Sheehan, PhD. Baltimore, Maryland

With the downfall of the ruling regime in Iran increasingly likely – and with virtually every major city in the country brimming with social unrest – calls for the Iranian opposition to unify abound. This begs the question: Is the political opposition to the ruling regime in Iran sufficiently united to mobilize and align its forces against the theocratic regime?

It is a valid question that requires a grasp of Iran's contemporary political history. Even more crucial is an understanding of the substantive differences between opposition movements and the corresponding influence operations employed by Iranian authorities to cast their opposition as fragmented – deliberate schemes designed to imply the absence of a unified front and a dim prospect for political change.

Though some Iran analysts argue that there is lack of unity among Iranian opposition movements and consider this to be a major, if not the primary, impediment to overthrowing the regime, others take a slightly different view. While there is little dispute that unity among dissident groups is helpful, it is equally important to acknowledge that the mantra of "everyone together" without a clear sense of the principles around which unity of coalition can be forged is a defective strategy that is unlikely to result in the regime's collapse or, more importantly, a democratic outcome. The basis for a politically viable coalition that can be successful in toppling the clerical regime and establishing good governance is the clear articulation of the principles around which different opposition forces and parties can unite.

The History

During the 1979 Iranian revolution, the political vacuum created by the Shah's decimation of pro-democracy forces through imprisonment and execution led to the emergence of Ruhollah Khomeini as the de facto leader of that revolution. Khomeini called for unity without describing what the parties were to stand together for. He shrewdly but cleverly understood that after the Shah's regime crumbled and power was transferred, he could dominate the future political direction of the country largely unchecked.

The ambiguity served Khomeini politically and was a clear shortcoming of that transformational event that eventually led to the political dominance of the clergy and their protectors in the soon-to-be formed Islamic Revolutionary Guards Corps (IRGC).

The popular revolution of 1979 was successful in unseating the Shah and the monarchy, but Khomeini's political grip on that massive social upheaval brought the same mindset of one-party authoritarian rule embedded with messianic characteristics. The republic in the so-called "Islamic Republic" became a meaningless prop for deflecting criticism of Khomeini's religious dictatorship, including his entourage of supporting clergy and personal army in the IRGC.

Genuine Opposition

In the aftermath of the 1979 revolution, Massoud Rajavi, the head of the leading anti-Shah opposition movement, the Mujahedin-e Khalq (MEK), gradually and methodically pushed back on Khomeini's then influential leadership. The MEK promoted a republican democracy and shunned the demagogic use of the term "Islamic" or the infusion of religion into the political system or process. Eschewed by Khomeini and his followers, the MEK's criticism was that Khomeini's political direction was towards absolute rule and therefore absolute corruption of power and religion.

The MEK's repeated attempts to thwart such an outcome by participating in the initial political process, while criticizing the Khomeini regime, were met with a fierce crackdown in June 1981.

The result was massive anti-government demonstrations by democratic activists, overwhelmingly from the MEK, and an ensuing massacre of these pro-democracy forces. June 1981 became a turning point in Iran's post-1979 revolutionary history insofar as Khomeini demonstrated that he would not tolerate any legitimate opposition to his rule – a decision that delegitimized his regime and paved the way for the impending struggle between the Iranian resistance and the regime to this day.

From June 1981 onwards, the word "opposition" took on a new meaning in Iran: anyone seeking to abolish the illegitimate regime and establish a new democratically inclined political system. Such an opposition was formed in Tehran on July 20, 1981, in a coalition of different political forces that was soon joined by representatives from various ethnic and religious minorities. The new coalition was named the National Council of Resistance of Iran (NCRI) and shortly thereafter its leaders and some members relocated to France – where they set up a parliament in exile – due to persecution that made it impossible to lead the resistance from inside the country.

Nevertheless, references to oppositionists came to include imprecise political language inclusive of internal factions seeking "reform" without legitimate political dissent that was outlawed by the Islamic Republic. Today, it is increasingly unnecessary to explain why the regime cannot be reformed and easy to bear witness to universal rallying cries like "Death to Khamenei" and "Hardliner, Reformer, the game is now over,' a chant repeated since 2017. But, in the final analysis, the only true marker for genuine opposition to the regime in Iran is its overthrow in its entirety – an objective that precludes engagement with internal factions, persons, and groups seeking concessions from, or dialogue, collaboration, or cooptation with the same.

Though Tehran peddles a false claim that some Iranian dissidents are content with regime modification, the only credible Iranian oppositionists are those committed to wholesale regime change. Blurring this distinction serves only to maintain the status quo.

Political Coalition

Political scientists have long understood that unity of purpose is indispensable to a successful opposition campaign against an entrenched totalitarian regime like the one in Iran that is deemed illegitimate by the general population.

The failure of opposition parties to unify and form a political coalition to successfully abolish the incumbent regime is frequently attributed to these factors: a successful "divide and conquer" strategy by the regime; oversized political ambitions of seemingly opposition personalities or groups that eventually succumb to regime cooptation; and most importantly, focused physical suppression and psychological warfare, on its most dangerous opposition, the MEK and NCRI.

Physical annihilation and demonization have been the two principal instruments used by the regime to achieve its goal. It has long been understood that any affiliation with, let alone expression of support for the MEK and NCRI, will be confronted with imprisonment, torture, and execution. Thousands of books, movies and websites have also been disseminated to spread disinformation and shape the popular discourse, inside Iran and around the world about the MEK.

This is hardly surprising. Following its decision to force the MEK underground after the revolution, the clerical regime realized that its primary threat was from the "overthrow" camp – the MEK and the NCRI. Those that contend that the monarchists were also seeking to topple the regime overlook the fact that monarchism as a political idea never had a serious political future, organization, or posture against the regime since its disgraceful fall from power with the removal of the Shah. A short historical review of the period suggests that the only consequential and compelling alternative to the regime came by way of the MEK and NCRI.

Anti-MEK Strategies

In the 1990's the regime began to devise a sophisticated anti-opposition strategy aimed at weakening what it considered its main foe. It divided its opponents into two camps: (1) those it believed harbored the intent and ability to topple the regime, namely the MEK and NCRI and (2) those it believed it could coax into criticizing these groups.

The goal was simple: to lure the regime's opponents into becoming what amounted to regime supporters by enlisting them in the repetition of allegations hurled at the MEK and NCRI.

By distancing itself from these groups, it allowed these individuals and groups to do the regime's bidding. Iran's Ministry of Intelligence and Security (MOIS) coined the 80/20 rule stating that phony opponents, who would come to receive the regime's quiet favor, could criticize the regime eighty percent of the time provided they attacked the MEK and NCRI on specific regime-devised allegations twenty percent of the time. Four decades later, the theocracy continues to be fixated on its nemesis, the MEK.

From his earliest days, Khomeini and his successors demonstrated a remarkable penchant for projecting their twisted values and indiscretions onto their enemies. In the 1980's, when the brutal torture of political prisoners came to light and caused a furor even within the seemingly pro-regime clergy, Khomeini shrieked "they torture themselves to accuse us of torture." Today, when the regime murders defenseless and innocent protesters, they categorize the casualties as "suicides" and go so far as to force relatives to attest or suffer persecution themselves.

Attacking the MEK and NCRI with regime-made allegations (from ridiculous claims that it is a cult, to false assertions that it has participated in human rights abuses against fellow Iranians, to unfounded assertions that the group has sided with enemies of the Islamic Republic including Iraq, Saudi Arabia, the United States, Israel, and a host of other actual or perceived enemies) constitute clear markers and coded language that the attackers are amenable to cooptation or perhaps cooperation by the regime.

Conclusion

This chapter examined the extent to which opposition movements in Iran can be best understood through the lens of the ayatollahs' concerted efforts to maintain the status quo by distinguishing between groups they deem lawful and those they deem unlawful, i.e., those they see as committed to unthreatening and ineffectual reforms versus those they view as an existential threat.

The fact of the matter is that few opposition groups have put their cards squarely on the table by committing to the goal of regime overthrow and a political platform to achieve it. The MEK and NCRI have called for a fully-fledged secular democracy and operationalized precisely what this will entail. By contrast, many other "oppositionists" inside the country, as well as those in exile, have been more circumspect in calling for limited procedural reforms – from the extension of some civil liberties and political rights to the release of political prisoners. But rarely is the principle of *Velayat-e Faqih* (governance of the most learned scholar) that is enshrined in the 1979 constitution ever challenged. This effectively leaves the regime's Supreme Leader with the ultimate power to control the courts, the police, the military, and critical organs of government, from the ministries of oil and foreign affairs to the Council of Guardians (a committee that can veto candidates for office and stop parliamentary legislation).

History suggests that authoritarian governments fall when populations coalesce around shared principles and a common cause presented by an opposition that has closed ranks. In Iran, where the experience of 1979 looms large, and the people are sufficiently politically sophisticated not to fall for another form of despotism, a sensible approach is not to defer discussion of democratic governance and a future republic to a later date but to bake it into the criteria for unity. A transparent and clear-cut position by all Iranian political forces coming out in opposition to the regime that presents a guaranteed democratic future for Iranian society is the only option that can gain traction. By understanding the influence operations employed by Iranian authorities, including the MOIS, and the credible basis for opposition unification, policymakers will be in a better position to appreciate the nature of viable opposition to the regime that merits international support.

Hallmarks of an Alternative

By Alejo Vidal-Quadras, Barcelona, Spain

The unity of opposition forces seeking to overthrow the regime and forming an alternative is one of the essential pillars of resistance against a dictatorship, especially the religious fascism ruling Iran. The existence of an alternative is an imperative for advancing the struggle to overthrow the regime and secure victory for a people who are willing to pay the price for the struggle. Conversely, the absence of an alternative can cause a revolution to fail or be diverted from its optimal path. The alliance of the forces participating in the revolution can already be seen on the streets of Iran. This writing intends to assess the characteristics of an alternative around which an alliance or coalition of movements willing to overthrow the ruling regime can be formed.

Attributes

An alternative to the ruling regime can be recognized by certain characteristics without which no group or coalition can be described as an alternative. These characteristics correlate to the historical, political, and social realities of Iran. Some of the most significant attributes that a viable alternative for the future of Iran needs to have follow:

1. Organization and structure

2. Domestic and international support

3. Competent leadership and a clear plan of action for the future

4. Pluralism

5. Rejection of any kind of dictatorship

1. Organization and structure:

To advance the political struggle, it is necessary for the alternative to have an organization that has optimal internal cohesion, leadership and a network of members and supporters both inside and outside Iran. Such an organization will enable the alternative to mobilize various cross-sections of the people, and to rely on its extensive network to advance the struggle against the ruling regime. It can lead, guide, and grow the protests and anti-regime activities of the people. It can act as an engine for change.

In the absence of such an organized entity, the struggle will not reach its objectives, and even if the regime is overthrown, will likely deviate from a path that leads to a democratic government of the people, for the people, and by the people. The 120-year history of the struggle of the Iranian people contains bitter experiences in this regard. During the August 19, 1953, coup against the nationalist and popular government of Dr. Mohammad Mosaddegh, led by the United States and Britain, in collusion with the Shah's court and with the cooperation of the reactionary clergy, Mosaddegh's government lacked a coherent and activist grassroots organization to counteract the coup makers.

Similarly, following the overthrow of the Shah in 1979, democratic organizations were not able to challenge Khomeini, who had hijacked the leadership of the revolution largely due to the Shah's bloody repression and execution and imprisonment of democratic leaders. The mullahs had a long history of collaborating with the Shah's secret police, SAVAK, before the 1979 revolution started. Khomeini and his network of mullahs diverted the revolution from its intended democratic goal and imposed a darker dictatorship than the Shah's.

The presence of democratic organizations can also prevent the emergence of pseudo alternatives aligned with the former dictatorship of the Shah or "reformist" currents within the current ruling system, both tainted by a dictatorial past and beliefs.

The alternative can leverage its organization and its extensive network inside the country to mobilize people to advance the fight against the repressive apparatus of the regime, weaken, and eventually topple it. It can disclose intelligence about unpatriotic policies and activities of the regime that are to the detriment of Iranians and the world such as its policy of exporting terrorism, nuclear weapons and ballistic missiles programs, and the production and export of drones and other destructive weapons used to kill people in other countries, to name a few.

2. Domestic and international support:

Direct polling and gauging of people's aspirations and votes in a dictatorship is obviously not possible. Therefore, in the era of repression, the only reasonable basis for the legitimacy of any movement or group is the price they pay for freedom and the level and quality of resistance they put up against dictatorship. One of the best means for discerning a political movement's popularity and acceptance in society is to refer to the statistics of affiliated martyrs and prisoners.

Such a popular base is imperative for an alternative not only inside Iran but also internationally with political recognition and support. In the final analysis, it is the people of Iran who are the main drivers of change, and without their support, no organization or movement can claim to be an alternative to the reigning dictatorship.

Popular support requires and emerges from deep historical roots, a record of struggling for freedom and democracy inside the country, and vibrant links with different sectors of society, especially the intelligentsia, and the middle and lower classes.

Experience derived from recent history in Iran's regional neighborhood has shown that imported alternatives that lack popular support and social legitimacy, jetting back to claim power after the downfall of an incumbent regime, cannot be viable alternatives. They will resort to repression of the people and increased reliance on various foreign actors to maintain their power. The bitter experience of transformations from repressive and puppet regimes in the past 50 years, both in the Middle East and in other countries, confirms this conclusion.

An alternative cannot gain the confidence of the people and win over a resilient base of social support without paying the necessary price for defying the brutal dictatorship that it aims to replace with democratic ideals. An alternative must be ready and able to overcome tremendous adversities, agonies, obstacles, misfortunes, and tribulations during its struggle. This is a necessary test of its genuineness and dedication to democratic principles and slogans. It is also an extremely vital element for gaining people's trust in it.

As the vanguard of the struggle, an alternative should pay a higher price to advance the struggle. It cannot shirk this intrinsic responsibility. From a historical perspective, too, such a commitment and readiness to embrace the pains of the struggle on the part of leaders and political organizations has both revealed and unlocked the path for people to show agency in achieving their rights and liberties. The history of Iran over the previous decades has produced many leaders who are considered as national symbols and heroes, serving as role models for future generations.

Outside Iran, an alternative should carry the support of the exiled community and be able to mobilize them to echo the voice of the people inside the country.

From an international point of view, any movement or group that claims to be an alternative should have international status, legitimacy, and recognition. It should garner the support of personalities, parties, legislators, and current and former officials belonging to all political persuasions around the world. For change and revolution in any country to be successful requires the political and moral support of democracy and freedom advocates around the world because of the close-knit fabric of human societies in the modern age. Without such a requisite it would be incredibly difficult – if not impossible – to bring about a democratic transformation, and it would require a much higher cost in human suffering and blood.

While a country's own citizens and leading political organizations play the defining role in the outcome of a struggle for freedom from dictatorship and realizing democratic governance, the role of the international community in accelerating or decelerating the process of change cannot be ignored. For example, the political appeasement of the regime by the West over the past four decades has been one of the most important impediments for decelerating the revolution and the overthrow of the clerical regime. The high price for this has been paid by the Iranian people and their resistance movement. International recognition and support will act as a future barrier to potential unproductive foreign interventions. At the same time, it will facilitate friendly and mutual relations based on the principle of non-interference in the internal affairs of all sides, ensuring peaceful relations within the framework of international law that can empower Iran to play its historical and constructive role in the Middle East and globally.

3. Competent leadership and a clear plan of action

The alternative to the ruling regime in Iran must have a competent and reliable leader who has a proven capability during the long and arduous struggle. Failed contemporary revolutions either going astray or being suppressed, including the 1979 revolution or the 2009 uprising in Iran, lacked precisely this attribute and proves its importance. A competent leadership must be willing to take risks to advance the struggle and be ready to pay the price of the difficult decisions that are necessary at different stages. Leadership cannot allow itself to be intimidated by the prevailing balance of power and should not sacrifice principles for the sake of short-term political benefits.

A viable alternative must have a clear plan of action for the future. This plan should provide solutions for major issues and challenges of society, guarantee individual and social rights and freedoms, women's rights, the rights of ethnic and religious minorities, address economic development and progress, ensure an independent judicial system, and have a clear foreign and environmental policy, to name a few.

The alternative should be capable of immediately implementing the plan after the overthrow of the regime and the establishment of a new government. In other words, specific programs and plans to be implemented while the new government organizes the holding of elections for the establishment of the Constituent Assembly and drafting the constitution of the new republic must be preannounced.

Postponing the announcement of such a platform to after the transfer of power would set the stage for betraying the pronounced ideals of a revolution, something that happened when Khomeini seized power. Prior to the 1979 revolution, whenever Khomeini was asked about his plans regarding various issues, he would slyly say that he will announce such plans after the revolution's victory. This untransparent and dishonest approach allowed him to impose a religious dictatorship by turning his back on previously announced vague promises.

4. Pluralism

An alternative must include representatives from an array of political tendencies and persuasions within society. The governing principle of such an alternative is pluralism and the ability to represent various political ideas and groups across the political spectrum, including left, liberal, conservative, people of faith and secularists. It should also represent Iran's ethnic minorities, including Baluchis, Kurds, and Arabs, and have specified and ratified plans for asserting and guaranteeing their rights.

During the 57-year reign of the Pahlavi monarchy (Reza Khan and his son Mohammad Reza) and the subsequent 43 years that the mullahs have been in power, only the dominant political point of view enjoyed any stake in power, and other political viewpoints and ethnic and religious minorities were denied their right in determining their destiny, severely suppressed and at times completely removed from the scene altogether. Only by accepting political diversity and pluralism can a melting pot be created, where different points of view of various classes and social sectors can come together and democratically and peacefully engage in dialogue. Iran is a country that has historically been a collection of different political tendencies, ethnicities, and religions, and in the last century, no government has respected the people's rights and views, leaving a democratic void that only such an approach can fill.

5. Rejection of any kind of dictatorship

Any political movement or coalition that wants to be considered as an alternative for the future of Iran must have clear boundaries with all types of dictatorship and authoritarianism, and it must necessarily have emerged from the revolution of the Iranian people against the Shah's dictatorship that promoted the ideals of freedom and independence.

As already discussed, in the era of dictatorship, when there is no possibility for the free and democratic expression of people's wishes, a true alternative derives its legitimacy from the level of its resistance to the ruling dictatorship. Purporting to speak against the regime does not automatically grant a person or movement, especially outside of Iran, alternative status.

If any individual or organization advocates for an authoritarian regime like the previous overthrown monarchy or one of its altered versions, they do not qualify as an alternative to dictatorship. Therefore, individuals or groups who seek to reinstate the overthrown monarchy or "reform" the religious dictatorship ruling

Iran cannot be part of the coalition that is supposed to be an alternative to the current regime.

Rejecting the former monarchical dictatorship is a major criterion because since the monarchy in Iran has always been intertwined with dictatorship and authoritarianism. Naïve comparisons of such a monarchy with the royals in England or in some Nordic or European countries is a false analogy. Monarchical systems in the latter countries after many centuries of political struggle, revolution, and reform, have a purely ceremonial role, and it is the people's elected representatives that wield actual and practical power in running these countries' affairs. In stark contrast, the course of developments in Iran has shown that over time, the rule of the Shah not only stymied reforms, but it took on increasingly authoritarian characteristics while devolving into one-party rule. Members of the parliament in such a system were not real representatives of the people. Rather, they served to rubber stamp the policies and whims of the monarch and his court. The history of the monarchy in Iran is not like the United Kingdom for example. It parallels more that of France, where the monarchical system was overthrown and abolished by the French Revolution.

The Pahlavi monarchy seized power through a coup against genuine constitutionalists. Seyyed Zia Tabatabai's coup d'état with British support in 1925 installed Reza Khan, a Cossack officer, to the throne. His son, Mohammad Reza Pahlavi, was crowned in 1941 following the forced exile of Reza Shah to South Africa by the Allies during World War II. Then in 1953, an American-British coup against the nationalist government of Dr. Mosaddegh returned Mohammad Reza Pahlavi to the throne.

During the reign of Reza Khan, originally as the prime minister and later as the king, all the democratically inclined freedom movements of the Iranian people, including the Jangal (Jungle) movement under the leadership of Mirza Kuchak Khan Jangli in Gilan, northern Iran (1915-1921), and the movement led by Mohammad Taqi Khan Pessian in Khorasan, northeastern Iran (1921), were violently suppressed. His son, Mohammad Reza Shah, created a one-party system in Iran - the Rastakhiz (Resurrection) Party. He suppressed not only liberal and moderate parties, such as the National Front and the Freedom Movement, but also revolutionary organizations like the Mujahedin-e Khalq (MEK) who are of the Muslim faith, and the Marxist Fedayeen. By silencing all dissenting voices, he paved the way for the hijacking of the revolution by Khomeini and his network of mullahs.

The quick pace and interdependence of historical, political, and social developments throughout the world, and at a time of great technological advances, make demands for a return to previous dictatorial and authoritarian systems of rule oxymoronic and obsolete.

National Council of Resistance of Iran (NCRI)

If we grant the five features outlined above as the constituent elements of an alternative, my experiences and familiarly with the National Council of Resistance of Iran (NCRI) and the Mujahedin-e Khalq (MEK) have convinced me that in the context of existing political realities in Iran, there is only one movement that satisfies virtually all these characteristics, granting it the status of a viable alternative to the religious tyranny ruling Iran. Among other things, I am basing this conclusion on extensive research about the NCRI/MEK as well as meetings and discussions with their officials and members in Ashraf-1 in Iraq before they were relocated to Albania and Europe.

The first feature was having the organization and being structured to survive the suppression and to operate effectively in such an environment. As the principal organization within the NCRI, the MEK stands out for its network and its resistance units inside Iran.

The current uprising in Iran cannot be separated from its past and forty years of relentless fighting in every sphere, political, social, publicity, military, etc. The MEK has been at the forefront of these campaigns. For example:

- The imprisonment and torture of hundreds of thousands of people and the execution of tens of thousands of MEK members and supporters in the 1980s.

- The massacre of 30,000 political prisoners in 1988, some 90% of whom were affiliated to the MEK, which the Iranian people still view as the biggest crime of this regime.

- The fierce political campaign inside and outside of Iran against the illusion of reform from within the ruling theocracy, from the early 1980s until today. Now, not only the Iranian public, but also many politicians and Iran observers have reached the same conclusion that this regime cannot be reformed.

- The campaign to expose the regime's terrorist activities.

- Preventing the Iranian regime from arming itself with nuclear weapons by exposing its clandestine nuclear sites and projects.

One can also refer to the Resistance Units that are affiliated with the MEK and have been proliferating across the country, especially in recent years. These units have presented the people with new ways to resist against the regime on the ground. Now, the younger generation is advancing these methods nationwide.

In 2013, the Resistance Units began their campaign on a small scale by writing graffiti on walls against regime officials (including the slogan of "death to Khamenei"). Their activities ranged from simple to complex, from distributing leaflets and writing slogans to tearing down photos of regime leaders, chanting slogans in the streets, and torching regime symbols. These units are formed in any neighborhood, school, factory, office, university, and elsewhere. They rely on a popular support base that has thwarted the regime's efforts to eliminate them.

In July 2021, one thousand Resistance Units joined the Iranian Resistance's annual Free Iran World Summit online. In 2022, their number had swelled to 5,000 and they linked up to the Summit.

The units were instrumental in the uprisings of 2017 and 2019, and they led the uprising and slogans in many cities. At the same time, they provided real-time and detailed reports on the uprising in different cities and regions. Based on the information these units communicated from inside the country, the Iranian Resistance announced that 1,500 protesters had been killed during the November 2019 uprising, which was later confirmed by the regime. The Resistance also published the names of 900 of the victims.

The Resistance Units played an important role in providing accurate and continuous information during the outbreak of the Coronavirus epidemic. By regularly checking hospitals and cemeteries and obtaining and disclosing internal communications of the regime's agencies, these units were able to inform the people of Iran and the world about the disastrous human toll of the regime's criminal mismanagement of the Covid-19 epidemic in Iran.

In recent years, the Resistance Units have spread a new culture among the young generation, i.e., the culture of resistance, by linking the young generation to the 40-year nationwide resistance against the mullahs' regime. A generation that was not born in the 1980s is now being inspired by the resistance the MEK put up in those years and the price it paid during the massacre of 1988.

The state media and officials have constantly emphasized the role of the MEK and specially these resistance units.

NCRI structure

The NCRI has a coherent structure and organization, a well-known leadership, a clear and unambiguous platform, a nationwide network within the country thanks to its pivotal member the MEK, and a diverse coalition that includes a wide range of political tendencies and prominent personalities. It also has extensive bipartisan support internationally.

The principles that the NCRI adheres to, which have been proclaimed since 1981, reject past dictatorships as well as the status quo. It promotes a future based on two original principles, namely freedom and independence. Another principle is the equality of all in the eyes of the law. For this reason, the NCRI has declared since the outset that it believes in a free and democratic Iran where no one is deprived of equal rights or granted special privileges based on racial, religious, or family affiliations. Therefore, it rejects both the monarchical and religious dictatorships and instead seeks a democratic republic.

The NCRI's goal is to establish freedom, democracy and a republic based on the separation of religion and state and democratic standards, where all people enjoy equal rights.

Since the outset, the NCRI has announced its views and plans regarding the main issues facing Iranian society. Among them are its plans for Kurdish autonomy within the framework of Iran's territorial integrity, gender equality in all arenas, religious freedoms, and denial of any privileges to specific religions or beliefs.

In addition, the NCRI has presented a plan entitled "National Solidarity Front" based on three principles. It considers these as the foundational principles for unity among all the republican forces that strive to overthrow the religious dictatorship. These three principles are: Rejection of the religious dictatorship in its entirety; The establishment of a republic; And the separation of religion and state. The plan contains no special privileges for the NCRI and its members. The plan accepts divergence of points of view even with respect to issues that the Iranian Resistance considers as extremely important. These are the minimum considerations that are necessary to craft a united coalition to ensure the establishment of a truly democratic republic based on free elections and a popular constitution.

The slogans of the people of Iran that echo in the streets of different cities these days are manifestations of these demands, especially the slogans of "Death to Khamenei," "Death to the principle of Velayat-e Faqih (absolute clerical rule)," and "Death to the oppressor, be it the Shah or the Supreme Leader," and " Neither monarchy nor the Supreme Leader, yes to democracy and equality."

The Ten-point plan presented by Maryam Rajavi,[1] the President-elect of the National Council of Resistance of Iran, at the European Council in 2006, outlines the NCRI's plans for the future of Iran.

The mere presentation or announcement of a platform does not mean that it will be implemented in the future. Rather, a credible alternative must demonstrate in practice that it is and will continue to be committed to its plans. A cursory review of the NCRI's actions and conduct over the past 40 years shows that it is committed to this platform in action and practice while it has remained in the opposition.

For example, when the NCRI talks about equality between men and women in its platform, it implemented such an outlook in practice before anyone else. About 57% of the members of the NCRI are women. The President-elect is a woman, and the main member organization, the MEK, is led by women. Or, when the NCRI declares that it believes in a non-nuclear Iran, it has taken action and exposed the mullahs' nuclear projects[2]. These revelations have acted as the main obstacle for the regime to obtain a nuclear bomb.

In addition, during more than four decades of rule by the clerical regime, it is no secret that most of the political prisoners slain during the struggle for freedom have been affiliated with the MEK. More than 100,000 members and supporters of this organization, including 30,000 who were killed in the massacre of political prisoners in the summer of 1988,[3] have given their lives for the resistance against the mullahs' regime.

The NCRI and MEK have a wide network of supporters around the world. More than any other group and by a wide margin, they have carried out extensive activities to inform the world about the severe violation of human rights in Iran, and to garner the support of

---

[1] "Plan for future Iran in 10 points." Maryam-rajavi. https://www.maryam-rajavi.com/en/viewpoints/plan-for-future-of-iran/.
[2] "Iran's Nuclear Weapons Program." Ncr-iran. https://www.ncr-iran.org/en/news/inside-source-reports/iran-s-nuclear-weapons-program/.
[3] "The 1988 Massacre of 30,000 Political Prisoners in Iran - NCRI." https://www.ncr-iran.org/en/1988-massacre-of-political-prisoners-in-iran/

parliaments and international political dignitaries for the people of Iran.

Among the NCRI's activities have been the organization of hundreds of annual meetings, gatherings, and protests, and holding massive annual rallies - known as " Free Iran World Summit"[4] - that are attended by more than 100,000 people, including hundreds of prominent political figures from the United States, Canada, Europe, Arab countries, Australia, and other countries. In their speeches, these dignitaries voice support for the people and resistance of Iran. The NCRI also conducts extensive activities and meetings with hundreds of parliamentarians and political figures around the world. These are but a short summary of the vast activities conducted by the NCRI and its extensive support network around the globe.

The dazzling results of these wide-ranging activities have been comprehensive disclosure about the regime's crimes and human rights violations and the ratification of 69 UN resolutions condemning human rights violations in Iran; the advancement of the global Justice Movement campaign for the victims of the 1988 massacre of political prisoners; support from majorities in national parliaments of European countries; majority backing in the US House of Representatives and the US Senate; and support from thousands of political figures, jurists, artists, Nobel Prize laureates, and hundreds of non-governmental human rights organizations, who have expressed their solidarity with the Iranian people and their resistance movement.

Conclusion

A political alternative is not something that can be spontaneously created overnight. As a viable alternative, the NCRI has grown deep roots during an arduous and long battle against the ruling religious

---

[4] "Iran Liberation - NCRI." Ncr-iran. https://www.ncr-iran.org/en/publications/iran-liberation/.

tyranny. This is a coalition that has defied the religious fascism, has developed a structure and organization, created a plan, and paid the price for resistance day after day. During all these tumultuous years, even as the conditions have become more difficult, the NCRI's commitment and perseverance have strengthened. It has remained loyal to its values and to that which it rejects as authoritarianism and dictatorship, past or present. It has remained wholly dedicated to democratic and freedom-loving principles and values, protecting these ideals from assaults waged by the enemy.

The ruling regime, on the other hand, tries to present its own narratives consistently, both in rhetoric and in action. Recently, the deputy of the regime's judiciary revealed that there is not a single meeting with European countries in which Tehran fails to raise the issue of pressuring the MEK and the Iranian resistance. It has also waged a massive psychological war and demonization campaign across the world against this movement. More than a thousand books, and hundreds of movies and TV series, have been produced to confront this alternative. Moreover, during the last 40 years, the slogans of "Death to the Hypocrites [MEK]," have never stopped to echo in the official meetings of the Iranian regime, or its Friday prayers all over the country, or its parliamentary sessions. Even a small percentage of such propaganda is not waged against any other movement.

If it were not for such dogged determination to stand up to religious fascism at any cost in all cultural, social, and political aspects, the fate of the Iranian people today would have been radically worse off, particularly because the tyrannical and blood-thirsty regime would have secured its dominance with no serious contenders on the scene.

The history of this resistance movement, which is full of critical chapters and high-risk and consequential decisions, has today brought the regime to such a vulnerable and shaky crossroad, defined by desperation in the face of an uprising and an alternative that will secure the regime's demise and a democratic future for the

Iranian people. The alternative presented by the Iranian resistance is now in a position of maximum advance.

The proven capabilities and competencies of the National Council of Resistance of Iran during its battle against the mullahs' regime, as well as its success in preserving the culture of struggle and liberty, means that a long series of issues and problems impacting the fate of the people and the revolution have their solution in this alternative. The existence of this alternative and the overthrow of the regime will guarantee peace, stability, unity, and territorial integrity of the country on the one hand, and the fundamental rights and liberties of the Iranian people, on the other. Such unity and its promise can already be seen in the slogans chanted by the Iranian people, including "From Zahedan to Tehran, I sacrifice my life for Iran" or "From Kurdistan to Tehran, I sacrifice my life for Iran."

Regime Tactics

By Struan Stevenson, Edinburgh, Scotland

The uprising and its longevity have exposed the regime's intrinsic vulnerability and desperation to end or at least reduce the power of the unrest. At the time of writing, these unprecedented protests have expanded to at least 280 cities. Over 700 people have been killed and more than 30,000 have been arrested by the regime. Significantly, virtually all social sectors and demographics have voiced their opposition to the regime in one way or another, demonstrating the geographical breadth and social depth of frustration and utter disenchantment with the status quo. These circumstances have shaken the regime to its core, exponentially raising the probability of its overthrow. They have also put the spotlight on the regime's main viable alternative, the National Council of Resistance of Iran (NCRI) and its major constituent, the Mujahedin-e Khalq (MEK).

Naming the main actor

Amid the grim realities for the regime in Iran and the social, political, and economic crises that have fueled the flames of unrest, a critical element has bolstered the uprising. The organized opposition, in the form of the MEK and particularly its Resistance Units inside Iran, has been instrumental in inspiring, leading, providing logistical support, and ensuring the persistence of the protests. An increasing number of regime officials and media outlets are alive to this reality and have publicly warned about the growing influence and reach of the MEK and its Resistance Units, particularly among the younger generation and women.

The Supreme Leader Ali Khamenei's main envoy within the Islamic Revolutionary Guard Corps (IRGC), said in November that nearly 50 of the primary "leaders" of the uprising arrested by the regime are MEK sympathizers.[1] Mostafa Pour-Mohammadi, a member of the Death Commission during the 1988 massacre and former minister of interior and judiciary, admitted as far back as July 2019: "There has not been a single incident of destruction [against the regime] over the past 40 years in which the MEK has not had a leading role. We have not yet settled the score with the MEK. ... We are going to deal with every single one of them. We are not joking."[2]

The rapid expansion of MEK Resistance Units has long been on the regime's radar. In 2019, the then-Intelligence minister Mahmoud Alavi reported: "Over the past year, 116 teams ("Resistance Units") associated with the MEK have been dealt with."[3] In May 2019, Tehran's Revolutionary Court sentenced an MEK activist Abdullah Ghassempour to death, while sentencing several others to imprisonment on charges of supporting the MEK.[4]

On a number of occasions, no less an authority than the Supreme Leader Ali Khamenei himself has publicly lambasted the MEK as the main organizer and leader of the nationwide protests. For example, in the midst of protests in 2020, Khamenei criticized Albania for hosting the MEK and said in a televised speech that the "small and sinister" country of Albania is now home to thousands of "treacherous" MEK members responsible for the unrest in Iran.[5]

---

[1] "50 leaders of the recent riots were MEK," *IRNA*, November 5, 2022. https://www.irna.ir/news/84933222

[2] Interview with Mosalas website, July 24, 2019. English transcript available at https://www.ncr-iran.org/en/news/human-rights/top-iran-official-defends-1988-massacre-vows-to-exterminate-the-mek/

[3] "Iran's Intelligence Minister Boasts of Wide-Ranging Successes." *Radio Farda*, April 20, 2019. https://en.radiofarda.com/a/iran-s-intelligence-minister-boasts-of-wide-ranging-successes/29892972.html

[4] "Four Prisoners of Evin Prison Sentenced to Death and Imprisonment." *HRANA*, May 22, 2019. https://www.en-hrana.org/four-prisoners-of-the-evin-prison-were-sentenced-to-death-and-imprisonment

[5] "Albanian Leaders Dismiss Khamenei's Purported 'Sinister' Smear." Radio Free Europe Radio Liberty, January 9, 2020. https://www.rferl.org/a/albanian-leaders-dismiss-khamenei-s-purported-sinister-smear/30368335.html

Khamenei added that the MEK "drew up plans" to lead the nationwide protests in November 2019. During the December 2017 protests, Khamenei, had again acknowledged the MEK's leading role, saying: "The MEK had prepared for this [protest] months ago. ... The MEK's media outlet had called for it."[6]

All roads to regime change

There is a reason why the regime's highest officials and security agencies have focused so intently on the MEK and its broadening activities. Over the past 40 years, the organization has been the first and only serious opposition movement calling for the entire theocracy's overthrow and advocating for regime change at the hands of the Iranian people themselves. This has been the MEK's consistent strategy since June 1981 when the clerical rulers massacred thousands of MEK supporters on the streets of Iran, leaving no other legitimate option but to call for the complete overthrow of the theocratic regime.

The 2022 uprising has shown in no uncertain terms that the MEK's strategy was indeed correct and all other proposed alternatives, including "civil disobedience" and inducing vague behavior change in the regime, have been wholly ineffective and futile. Only by aligning with the strategy deployed by the MEK and Resistance Units can other options prove effective. Today, young people in the streets of Tehran and other cities are calling for the regime's complete overthrow, attesting to the legitimacy and effectiveness of the MEK's slogans and strategies over the past four decades. In unison with the MEK's message, protesters are calling for regime change and democracy, explicitly rejecting both the previous monarchy and the current theocracy.

---

[6]The official website of Supreme Leader Ali Khamenei, January 9, 2018. http://english.khamenei.ir/news/5394/Recent-damage-inflicted-on-Iran-by-U-S-will-gain-a-response

Diversionary tactics

This explains why the regime views the MEK and the NCRI coalition as existential threats. Tehran has engaged in multi-faceted tactics against the organized resistance movement to weaken, marginalize and ultimately destroy it.

On the one hand, during previous uprisings, the MOIS tried to promote the slogan "Reza Shah, may your soul rest in peace" to convey the notion that protesters are inclined to support the return of the monarchy. By doing so, the regime sought to demoralize protesters by advocating for the previous infamous dictatorship. But the attempt quickly failed. Video footage capturing scenes of protests, for example in Isfahan, showed demonstrators exposing those who chant slogans as members of the paramilitary Basij. At the same time, eyewitness testimonies exposed this plan even more. For example, Hashem Khastar, a teachers' union representative who has spent a long time in Mashhad prison, called attention to attempts by the MOIS to promote monarchy over the MEK. He wrote:

"There is a sea of blood separating the regime and the MEK. Everybody knows that the biggest enemy of the regime is the MEK because it has an ironclad organizational prowess and as admitted by the rulers of the regime, they have been involved in all protests. On the contrary, the forces affiliated with the monarchists are incredibly scattered and unorganized. Therefore, the regime is trying to encourage dissidents to move towards the monarchists' camp. Meanwhile, it has sent infiltrators within their ranks, who express support for the Crown Prince and attack the regime, while simultaneously attacking the MEK. In other words, they identify the main enemy as the MEK rather than the Islamic Republic. To make these individuals appear as credible opponents of the regime, some of them may even be jailed for a while, so that they can acquire a more acceptable standing and safety net, to be able to advance their mission more effectively. Other individuals may fall unwittingly in the intelligence agents' trap and view the MEK, rather than the regime, as the primary enemy."[7]

He also wrote in a post on the social media application Telegram: "In April 2018, when the intelligence agents raided my garden, they asked me why I do not work with the Crown Prince Reza Pahlavi? Would you like us to call his mobile for you to talk to him? I said no."[8]

Syrianization myth

The regime also tries to decelerate the MEK's growing social reach by causing deviations when it comes to the protests' primary aims and core messaging. It does this by attempting to distort reality, disseminate fake news and fabricate a dominant narrative unfavorable to protesters. Tehran has promoted the message that if it were to be overthrown, Iran will risk becoming like Syria or Lebanon, especially considering the many ethnic and religious groups that comprise the country. "Civil war," "Breaking Iran into pieces," and "jeopardizing Iran's territorial integrity" are code words used by the regime to both discourage new acts of protest and to legitimize the suppression of ongoing ones.

On October 31, 2022, for example, the official IRNA news agency quoted the regime's foreign minister as saying that foreign entities are "plotting a civil war in Iran" and stressed that Iran's "territorial integrity" is in danger due to the nationwide protests. On November 18, a senior IRGC commander, Majid Arjomandfar, similarly underscored the "enemies' renewed attempts to break apart the Islamic Iran and sow the seeds of insecurity."[9] The daily *Kayhan* newspaper, close to the regime's Supreme Leader Ali Khamenei, said on November 26 while pointing to the protests: "The enemy wants more bloodshed to keep the country in emergency

[7] https://www.balatarin.com/permlink/2019/7/22/5139363
[8] https://www.balatarin.com/permlink/2019/7/30/5143336
[9] https://www.hamshahrionline.ir/news/720997

circumstances and in the end move Iran toward civil war."[10] And on November 23, the IRGC's political deputy said that the "enemy" carried out the recent "riots" in order to "create a Syrian scenario" in Iran.[11]

But in Iran, the ongoing nationwide protests encompass all class, gender, ethnicity, and religious beliefs. Slogans from Kurdistan in the west to Sistan-va-Baluchistan in the east show that this is not a battle among ethnicities or religious groups. It does not pit a social or political majority against a minority or vice versa. Rather, virtually everyone is rallying around the slogans of "Death to Khamenei" (overthrow), and "Death to the oppressor, be it the Shah or the Leader" (charting a path forward to a democratic republic). Therefore, the regime's hyperboles in this case are pure fiction simply designed to keep itself in power for as long as possible.

People across Iran, from Tehran, Isfahan and Mashhad, to Azerbaijan, Zahedan, and other cities in Baluchistan and Kurdish cities, chant slogans like "From Baluchistan to Tehran, I sacrifice my life for Iran," or "From Kurdistan to Tehran, I sacrifice my life for Iran." Therefore, it is clear that the progress of the uprising and the revolution against the entirety of the regime is leading to further expressions of unity and solidarity among Iran's ethnicities.

Demonization

Another attempt by the regime to confront the MEK is to strictly demonize, delegitimize, and invalidate the entire resistance movement inside and outside Iran. This sophisticated vilification campaign has been multi-faceted, unrelenting, well-funded and extensive as a matter of state policy. It relies on fabricated and well-orchestrated messaging and narratives promoted by "former members" of the MEK, guided commentary by fake "opponents" of

---

[10] https://www.hamshahrionline.ir/news/720997
[11] https://www.tasnimnews.com/fa/news/1401/09/03/2811443

the regime, and Tehran's burgeoning cyber army in the virtual world.

For years, the regime has employed the services of so-called former MEK members who have defected years or decades ago. According to a US Library of Congress report in December 2012: "From 1990–93, [the Iranian regime's Ministry of Intelligence and Security] MOIS recruited former members of the Mojahedin-e-Khalq (MEK)—also known as the People's Mujahedin of Iran (PMOI) or MKO— in Europe and used them to launch a disinformation campaign against the MEK. The Iranian government and its intelligence apparatus consider the MEK the most serious dissident organization with regard to the Revolution."[12] The report adds: "Ali Younesi, the former minister of intelligence and security, reported on state television in October 2004 that the ministry's Department of Disinformation had hired thousands of agents, including some former MEK members, to boost the department's function." [13]

The report draws attention to two clear cases regarding these so-called "former MEK members," publishing their pictures and revealing the MOIS policy in this regard: "The recruitment of a British subject, Anne Singleton, and her Iranian husband, Masoud Khodabandeh, provides a relevant example of how the MOIS coerces non-Iranians to cooperate. She worked with the MEK in the late 1980s. Masoud Khodabandeh and his brother Ibrahim were both members of the MEK at the time. In 1996 Masoud Khodabandeh decided to leave the organization. Later, he married Anne Singleton. Soon after their marriage, the MOIS forced them to cooperate by threatening to confiscate Khodabandeh's mother's extensive property in Tehran. Singleton and Khodabandeh then agreed to work for the MOIS and spy on the MEK."[14]

---

[12] "Iran's Ministry of Intelligence and Security: A Profile," A Report Prepared by the Federal Research Division, Library of Congress, under an Interagency Agreement with the Combating Terrorism Technical Support Office's Irregular Warfare Support Program, December 2012.
https://irp.fas.org/world/iran/mois-loc.pdf
[13] Ibid, pp: 1, 27.
[14] Ibid. p. 27.

Judicial and security officials in Europe have shown, based on concrete evidence, that these "former members" are involved in malicious activities and disinformation against the MEK guided strictly by the regime's intelligence and terrorist agencies. For example, Albania's police chief announced in October 2019 the disruption of a terrorist network controlled by the regime that intended to harm the MEK and its members.[15] He said Alireza Naghashzadeh, an agent of Iran's Ministry of Intelligence and Security (MOIS), was involved in this terrorist operation. Naghashzadeh identifies himself as a "former member" of the MEK. In April 2016, German authorities arrested Meysam Panahi, who claimed to be a former MEK member, for spying on the MEK and NCRI.[16] He was sentenced to over two years in prison. Court proceedings revealed that Panahi operated under orders from a senior intelligence officer based in Tehran and identified as Sajjad.

In 2022, the Albanian media reported that authorities had detained and interrogated 20 Iranian nationals on charges of espionage in the service of the regime's intelligence services.[17] These individuals were accused of "receiving money from Iran's secret services, the Qods Force and the IRGC to obtain information about the MEK in Albania." This ring was comprised of "former members" of the MEK recruited by the regime's intelligence service. Tellingly, the anti-MEK ring run out of Tehran and residing in Albania, was able to dupe or manipulate a dozen journalists from such news media sources as *The Guardian, Foreign Policy, The Independent, Der Spiegel,* MSNBC, and even the BBC and the *New York Times,* as well as others, to publish derogatory and outlandish accusations against the MEK.

---

[15] https://apnews.com/article/e785b07e18fb4648bf6a540b9ea6c1fe

[16]   https://www.dw.com/en/germany-charges-two-for-spying-on-irans-mek-on-behalf-of-iranian-intelligence/a-19175147

[17]   https://www.voxnews.al/english/aktualitet/dyshime-per-spiunazh-spak-kontrolle-ne-banesat-e-ish-anetareve-te-mek-i14299

The 80/20 rule

The regime's other method to demonize the MEK is using individuals who identify themselves as "opponents", to criticize the MEK. Cognizant of the fact that its own propaganda against the MEK would have little, if any, chance of success in undermining the Resistance's international standing, Tehran devised what is commonly known within the Iranian diaspora as the 80/20 rule for those who sought its favor.[18] This tactic means that so-called "opponents" focus eighty percent of their criticism on the obvious and unavoidable, including mild or implied criticism of the regime, in order to establish credibility. They then target the MEK for the remaining twenty percent of the time, pushing Tehran's propaganda line. This tactic is meant to lend a measure of credibility to the anti-MEK propaganda, supposedly because it is coming from those who at first glance cannot be dismissed as regime agents.

An example is Mehrdad Arefani. Sentenced by a Belgian court to a 17-year imprisonment term in February 2021 for his role in the attempted bombing of the NCRI annual gathering in 2018, Arefani started to cooperate with the regime while in prison in Iran. He was later sent to Europe. He claimed to be a poet, a human rights activist, and even an atheist in order to distance himself from the regime. He even launched a campaign against Iranians visiting Iran to gain credit as an opponent of the regime. He claimed to be a political sympathizer of the MEK and acted as a sleeper cell and intelligence asset of the regime for nearly 18 years. In a report to a Belgian tribunal, the Belgian State Security wrote: "The MOIS continues to portray the opposition in a negative light and describes them as terrorists. The MOIS is particularly active in the field of anti-MEK (Mujahedin-e Khalq, Iranian opposition group) propaganda in the European Parliament."

The ultimate objective of the regime's demonization and vilification campaign is to set the stage for the execution of terrorist plots

---

[18] https://www.tabletmag.com/sections/israel-middle-east/articles/new-york-times-iran-erdbrink.

against the Iranian Resistance. Arefani, for example, had carried out all his activities and preparations as the groundwork for a large-scale terrorist plot.

The cyber army

Finally, the regime uses its vast resources to deploy a cyber army as yet another prong in its demonization campaign against the MEK. According to a report by the Center for Strategic and International Studies on June 25, 2019,[19] three military organizations were playing leading roles in cyber operations: the Iranian Revolutionary Guard Corps (IRGC), the Basij, and Iran's 'Passive Defense Organization (NPDO).'"

In a striking admission in May 2022, Ruhollah Momen Nasab, a former commander of Tehran's cyber army, provided a glimpse of its operations and said: "We created new accounts on Twitter, using the persona of other Twitter influencers who were mainly counter-revolutionary activists. Ours just differed in a single character and was quite similar to the real one. We used the same picture and the same name, but everything was fake. Once created, we started our activities."[20]

On November 4, 2019, the regime posted fake stories about the MEK. It used a fake Twitter account of Alexis Kohler,[21] Secretary-General of the office of French President Emmanuel Macron in the Elysée Palace, claiming that "The Secretary-General of the French Presidency has announced that the People's Mojahedin (PMOI/MEK) will soon be driven from France." The next day, the Elysée denied this statement, adding that the senior official did not even have a Twitter account.

---

[19] https://www.csis.org/analysis/iran-and-cyber-power
[20] https://twitter.com/i/status/1508774815599153152
[21] https://www.ncr-iran.org/fr/communiques-cnri/international/iran-nouveau-cyber-scandale-du-regime-des-mollahs/

On December 10, 2020, Treadstone 71, a California-based independent cyber intelligence company, released details of an Iranian influence operation.[22] It said: "The IRGC Cyber Units triggered core team members with military precision aimed at the National Council of Resistance of Iran (NCRI) annual online conference. The IRGC, MOIS, and low-level Basij Cyber Units flooded Twitter with nearly one hundred twelve thousand tweets over sixty hours using hashtags and content intent on controlling the social media narrative."

More recently, in September 2022, Microsoft was asked to investigate a destructive cyber-attack against the Albanian government in mid-July. The tech giant said in a report: "The messaging, timing, and target selection of the cyberattacks bolstered our confidence that the attackers were acting on behalf of the Iranian government."[23] Microsoft added: "Ahead of the cyberattack, on June 6, Ebrahim Khodabandeh, a disaffected former MEK member posted an open letter addressed to Albanian Prime Minister Edi Rama warning of the consequences of escalating tensions with Iran. Invoking '[h]acking of Tehran municipal systems' and 'gas stations,' Khodabandeh claimed that the MEK was the source of 'sabotaging acts against the interests of the Iranian people [sic]' and argued that these constituted 'the hostile work of your government' and has caused "obvious enmity with the Iranian nation [sic].'"

The comprehensive and detailed Microsoft report also said: "In May 2021, at around the same time that Iranian actors began their intrusion into Albanian government victim systems, accounts for two anti-MEK social media personas, which do not appear to correspond to real people, were created on both Facebook and Twitter. The accounts largely post anti-MEK content and engage with the social media accounts of some of the individuals detailed above. These two accounts along with a third, older account, were among the first to promote posts from Homeland Justice accounts

---

[22]   https://www.ifmat.org/12/10/treadstone-releases-intelligence-advisory-iranian-influence-operations/

[23]   https://www.microsoft.com/en-us/security/blog/2022/09/08/microsoft-investigates-iranian-attacks-against-the-albanian-government/

on Twitter, and all three dramatically increased the rate of anti-MEK posts after the mid-July 2022 cyberattack became public."

Now that the instrumental and expanding role of the MEK and its Resistance Units have become increasingly threatening for the regime, Tehran has become even more focused on its demonization campaign against the movement. Persistent and systematic attacks and lies against the MEK are critical as far as the regime is concerned. Not least because the MEK has a leading role in organizing the protests. Moreover, the mullahs are keenly aware that the MEK and the NCRI are the most viable alternatives to their rule. During an unprecedented nationwide uprising, a weakened and desperate regime is utilizing every means at its disposal, including "former members," "opponents," and a cyber army to confront the MEK's rising popularity and organizational prowess in the hopes of countering the powerful tides of the uprising.

International Community's Role

By Robert Torricelli, Lambertville, New Jersey

The uprising of the Iranian people, which broke out on September 16, 2022, once again elevated the Iranian crisis into a major international headline. Girls and women challenged the ruling system, displaying unparalleled courage. Within a few hours, the protests against the murder of a young woman grew into an uprising against the entire regime, spreading all over the country.

The world is facing new realities in Iran, which accentuate the imperative to alter international policy towards it. What is needed is a thorough overhaul. The time for such change is now, not a year or six months or even a month from now. Change is long overdue.

William Shakespeare's "what's past is prologue" can be instructive here. When President Jimmy Carter addressed the Shah in Tehran on December 31, 1977, proclaiming "Iran, because of the great leadership of the Shah, is an island of stability in one of the more troubled areas of the world," he could not have even imagined that exactly one year later, in January 1978, the Shah would be forced to flee the country and in February, the monarchy would be overthrown permanently. Even in the fall of 1978, CIA analysts assessed that Iran was "neither at the revolutionary stage nor even at the pre-revolutionary stage." Such assessments surfaced even when the US had an embassy in Tehran and over 50,000 Americans were operating in various capacities across the country.

Similarly, in 2022, the uprising has taken Western governments and analysts by surprise. The conventional wisdom in Western capitals has been that the regime of the ayatollahs is virtually invincible and the prospect of regime change inconceivable.

Such thinking has served as the foundation of Western policy towards Iran for many years. On this basis, the only effective way to deal with the regime was to cajole and compromise with it. Ironically, the more the clerical regime intensified its repression inside Iran and its export of terrorism and insecurity abroad, the more the West sought to appease it.

In November 1979, for the first time in modern history, a government of one country took hostage the diplomats of another. Some 52 diplomats and foreign nationals were held hostage for 444 days by the Iranian regime. It claimed the hostage takers were students but they were, in fact, "Followers of Imam," the Supreme Leader's political party.

In subsequent years, further malevolent actions were taken by the regime. Besides the assassinations of opponents, the atrocities include: the killing of 241 American marines and 58 French soldiers and six peacekeeping civilians in Lebanon in October 1983; the hostage-taking of Western nationals in Lebanon; terrorist bombings in Europe throughout the 1980s; bombings in Arab countries, Africa and Latin America in the 1990s; and the horrific bombing of the Khobar Towers in Saudi Arabia in June 1996, which killed 19 and injured nearly 500 Americans. The Iranian regime's continuing terrorism, as well as its violent intervention in the Middle East, now, as in the past, has not been met with any serious countermeasures by the West. Even more disturbing, the West made conscious efforts to cover up or downplay the role of the Iranian regime in acts of terrorism.

On April 10, 1997, after a court in Germany explicitly emphasized the role of the highest officials of the Iranian regime in the murder of four opponents at the Mykonos restaurant in Berlin, European Union members recalled their ambassadors from Tehran, and the EU announced that it would not allow intelligence agents of the Iranian regime to set foot on European soil. But not even this half-hearted policy survived for long, with normal relations and concessions to the regime resuming in November of that year. Western policy has not improved since.

In 2018, the security services of Belgium, Germany, France and Luxembourg, in a joint operation, neutralized a bombing plot against the annual rally of the National Council of Resistance (NCRI) taking place in the suburbs of Paris. Supervised by Assadollah Assadi[1], a senior Iranian diplomat serving in an EU country, the regime's plan was to explode a bomb in the heart of Europe, at a rally attended by tens of thousands of ordinary Iranians as well as prominent dignitaries from Western countries.

In response, the European Union was content with placing two regime officials on the terrorist list without taking any concrete or meaningful actions against the regime as a whole. Even after the Antwerp court sentenced the diplomat to 20 years and his three accomplices to 17 and 18 years in prison, and even after documents and evidence presented in court showed that the bomb was brought to Europe in a diplomatic pouch from Iran, the Europe Union again refrained from taking any practical measures. Apparently, the Iranian regime has complete political immunity from the West.

Rationales for appeasement

Western governments of course would deny that they have a policy of appeasement towards Iran. Instead, in public, policy is rationalized by the claim that there is a moderate faction within the regime that can be the source of positive, if gradual, change in the regime's behavior. Every President, bar one, has been presented as a quiet opponent of the Supreme Leader. In the face of the President Mahmoud Ahmadinejad's close ties to the Supreme Leader, a new rationale emerged: the benefits to the West in reaching an agreement on Iran's nuclear program would outweigh other considerations. Agreed during the Presidency of Hassan Rouhani, the West hailed as a great achievement the nuclear agreement formally known as the Joint Comprehensive Plan of Action (JCPOA). At the same time, the West claimed its inaction against Iran's terrorism was actually a policy aimed at keeping the

---

[1] https://www.ncr-iran.org/en/iran-regime-diplomacy-of-terror/

"hardliners" in the regime at bay through rapprochement. Opponents of the policy were named "warmongers".

The West's claim that a moderate faction existed in Iran has been completely undermined by protests in Iran since 2017: the Iranian people chant, "Reformists, hardliners, the game is now over." During the current uprising, the population has shown that they despise the supposed "reformists" as much as the "hardliners," blaming the former for having long played the role of the regime's safety valve. Even Mohammad Khatami, hailed in the West as the most moderate of all Iranian Presidents, voiced support for the regime's policy of suppressing the uprising.

Another rationale presented by the West was that regime change was impossible in the context of Iran's military power. The presence of the Islamic Revolutionary Guard Corps (IRGC) in particular left no possibility of change by the people. Thus, the rational went, the only option was to wait for reform from within the regime. The rationale has its parallel in the 1970s when it was claimed that the strength of the military protected the Shah.

The IRGC will stand with Khamenei until the bitter end. However, no military force, regardless of its power, can withstand the will of its own population. In any case, the IRGC is riven with corruption, and, in the face of the uprising, with disenchantment, particularly among its mid-tier and lower-level personnel.

Still another rationalization of Western policy towards Iran is that the regime has a stable social base among the lower classes of society. This perception was shattered in November 2019 with the uprising of the lower classes. At that time, protesters set fire to thousands of regime-affiliated centers. These were the very "disadvantaged" people that the regime had claimed to be its core constituency. Of course, Khamenei suppressed the uprising by killing 1,500 people. But the world clearly observed the dissolution of the regime's base among underprivileged classes.

The final rationale deployed by the West is that having overthrown one despot, the Shah, in pursuit of democracy, and having been rewarded with another tyranny, the Iranian people do not desire another revolution. The current uprising invalidates this argument: the protestors shout, "This is no longer a protest, it is a revolution."

Behind the rationales lay political and economic interests, of course, but it is also worth examining the sophisticated operation that is the regime's lobby in the West. Individuals working under the cover of researchers and academics promoted the notion that there are moderate elements inside the regime. Ostensibly independent research projects have been funded by elements affiliated with the Iranian regime. Many universities in the US received such financial aid from the Alavi Foundation. Iran has also organized professional lobbies, such as NIAC in the United States. It is widely despised by Iranians.

The missing link

The missing link in Western, and especially American, policy towards Iran was the failure to listen to the voice of the Iranian people and the democratic opposition. This repeats the error committed during the Shah's era.

Worse, not only did Western governments not listen to the voice of the people, but in order to appease the mullahs, the main opposition, the MEK, was designated as a terrorist organization - by the US in 1997 at the request of the regime. The United Kingdom and the European Union followed suit a few years later. After a long legal battle, the Court of Appeal in the United Kingdom, the Court of Justice of the European Union, and finally the Court of Appeal of the District of Columbia in the US delisted the MEK, testifying to the legitimacy of the organization. However, the policy has had serious and longstanding impacts.

Less than two weeks after the MEK's listing in the US, I wrote the following to President Clinton:

"I write to bring to your attention a serious policy mistake in the making. On October 8, 1997, Secretary Albright issued a list of 30 groups designated as foreign terrorist organization. On that list were many groups which merited such designation. One that did not was the People's Mojahedin Organization of Iran (PMOI).

"Our country was born in resistance to oppression. Surely our foreign policy in its fight against terrorism can distinguish between political movements fighting to preserve their values and oppose tyrannical regimes and those which target innocent civilians. I have reviewed personally the intelligence purporting to justify the designation of the PMOI as terrorist and find it unpersuasive."

I added: "In designating the PMOI as a terrorist group, an anonymous 'senior Clinton administration official,' quoted in the Los Angeles Times, described the decision to include the PMOI in the list of designated groups 'as a goodwill gesture to Tehran and its newly elected moderate president, Mohammad Khatami.

"Whatever the message you were intending to send to Tehran, the one received is that the regime is justified in its murderous policies towards its own people and its neighbors in the region. The Iranian regime has applauded the designation by the United States of its principal opposition as terrorists but will not change its behavior in response to our 'goodwill gesture."

And I concluded by mentioning the negative repercussions of the decision for European allies: "Our allies in Europe, already eager to sacrifice principle to profits, will also read these recent decisions as evidence of a cynical duplicity in US policy: seeking to block their economic dealings with Iran while preparing the way for our own."

This policy has been harmful not only for the people of Iran but also for our national security. This mistaken policy, which was also adopted by Europe, effectively locked down the most serious lever for change in Iran, the organized opposition, for many years. It created a staging ground for the propaganda campaign of the Iranian regime and its lobby. The mullahs' tactics were complex, but at the same time easy to figure out. The attempts revolved around discrediting the organized opposition in order to make Western governments believe that, in the absence of a viable and democratic alternative, realpolitik dictates that they should simply come to terms with this regime. By blacklisting the MEK, Western countries facilitated and enabled the realization of the regime's core objectives.

A new policy?

What should be the new policy? The uprising of the Iranian people in recent months leaves no doubt that the dominant policy of the past should be discarded. Both America and European countries have condemned the Iranian regime and expressed sympathy with the protesters. Beyond that, at the initiative of Germany and Iceland, the United Nations Human Rights Council has approved the formation of a commission of inquiry regarding the deteriorating human rights situation in Iran. The US and some other Western countries have sought and succeeded to expel Iran from the UN Commission on the Status of Women. Some European and American officials have held symbolic meetings with several Iranian civil society activists abroad. The totality of these measures represents positive steps, but the West still seems hesitant to approach the focal point of the right policy towards Iran. What is necessary is not simply reforming the current policy, but a complete overhaul of it.

There is no need for military action by the West or any interference in Iran's internal affairs. The uprising of the Iranian people in the last three months showed that, contrary to the idea posed for many years in the West, the Iranian people are both willing and able to change the regime because they have proven that they are prepared to pay the price for change.

The US and, in my view, Europe must fundamentally change their policy in two respects. The first component is defined by changing the nature of the relationship with the regime. The idea of compromise and getting along with this regime should be abandoned once and for all. Applying limited pressure in the false hope of encouraging the Iranian regime to change its behavior continues to cast a shadow on Western policy towards Iran. This is the why the current policy relies on rhetoric and or symbolic actions when it comes to protests in Iran, rather than concrete practical actions, which would signal a shift in policy.

Europe and Canada have sanctioned many individuals, which is a step in the right direction, but it does not have a material impact in the way of holding to account those responsible for the killing of Iranian citizens and for sponsoring terrorism abroad. Western actors have refrained from designating the IRGC and the Iranian Ministry of Intelligence as terrorist organizations. The IRGC's blacklisting, particularly in light of its dominant role in Iran's economy, can have a real impact. Additionally, the MOIS actively plots terrorist operations on Western soil.

Another indicator of a shift in policy would be to trigger the snapback mechanism and to reinstate the six UN Security Council resolutions. According to agreements among involved parties to the nuclear deal, UN Security Council members cannot use their veto power to prevent the resumption of sanctions. Iran has demonstrably violated its obligations in the context of the Joint Comprehensive Plan of Action (JCPOA). America's withdrawal from the JCPOA in 2018 cannot be deemed as justification for Iran's violation of the agreement. In addition, by sending drones to Russia to kill the people of Ukraine, Iran has clearly violated UN Security Council Resolution 2231. Therefore, the failure to trigger the snapback mechanism would send a message to the Iranian regime that the West is still not serious about adopting a decisive policy towards it.

Still another component that is even more significant, and which is the missing link of Western policy, is acknowledging the objective realities of Iranian society and listening to the voice of the people and the opposition. A false hypothesis has been promoted by the regime's lobby, which claims there is no resistance movement or viable opposition in Iran. This is a product of the regime's lobbying in the West and the psychological warfare and extensive demonization campaign that the regime has been able to prolong for years against the MEK and the NCRI on the basis of past terrorist designations in the West.

By adopting a policy of appeasement, which included labelling the primary opposition as "terrorists," Western governments provided a suitable platform for the regime and its lobby to advance the policy of demonizing the Resistance, bolstering the claim that there is no alternative to the regime. As Vice President Mike Pence said in June 2022, the claim that there is no alternative to this regime is one of the biggest lies the regime has sold the world.

The MEK is a movement that has been subjected to the most severe forms of repression over the past 43 years. Tens of thousands of its members and supporters have been executed, and it remains to this day a forbidden name in Iran. On the international stage, the organization was blacklisted in the US and Europe in alignment with the policy of appeasement toward Tehran.

However, despite such tremendously arduous circumstances, the MEK has managed to overcome such obstacles while maintaining its cohesion. Today, both supporters and detractors agree on one thing, that the MEK remains to be the only organized and effective opposition force in Iran. The organization is a fixture in any major development in Iran and cannot be simply ignored.

A big mistake for the West would be to decide its policy towards the opposition based on whim. The long-term interests of the West demand that its current policies must correspond to the realities of Iran and not political wishes and hopes. Failure to do so defined the fundamental mistake committed by the West during the Shah's era. The West continued to support the monarchical dictatorship until its final moments, despite the preponderance of evidence regarding the Shah's crimes, including the torture and execution of opponents, simply because a dependent ruler was ideal for the US during the Cold War. But that same regime provided the breeding ground for the Ayatollahs to seize power by suppressing opposition forces and preventing the formation of democratic institutions.

In tandem with the outbreak and continuation of the 2022 protests in Iran, there has been a tangible sense of activism and advocacy among the Iranian diaspora. Those who were silent over the years for various reasons, including maintaining family ties, or protecting financial and commercial interests, and even preserving the option to travel to Iran, are now participating in anti-regime demonstrations abroad. Most of them have no political links to opposition groups. The development of political circumstances of the uprising will determine their future affiliations. Some figures have entered the scene more actively, which can all be positive. But political figures or groups in the Iranian diaspora can only be truly effective when they are organized, with this organized movement having a history and roots back in Iran itself.

Before the invasion of Iraq and the overthrow of the government at that time, with the help of the United States, various Iraqi individuals and groups were brought together, while in reality these groupings did not believe in common principles for running the country. It was a loose coalition created by the US and did not represent an authentic Iraqi partnership.

Many members of that coalition were affiliated with the Iranian regime, a fact that was proven during developments unfolding in the following years. Immediately after the fall of the Iraqi government, this coalition functioned in a disastrous manner despite all the help offered to it by the US and despite the presence of 180,000 American troops in that country.

Therefore, neither the US not any other foreign country should involve itself in forming a coalition for Iran. Forming such political coalitions should be an entirely Iranian enterprise.

In the early 2000s, and after the March 2003 invasion of Iraq, the MEK was based in the country. The Iranian regime, seeking to destroy the organized movement for decades, and thanks to an appeasement policy that had provided it a golden opportunity, was beginning its domination of Iraqi affairs in earnest by forming key alliances and recruiting and organizing mercenaries to do its bidding.

Women and men of the MEK, completely unarmed and defenseless, were the subject of unprecedented and gruesome terrorist and military assaults by the regime's mercenaries, during which hundreds of members were inhumanely slaughtered and scores more injured or maimed.

Yet the MEK survived as an organization by staying laser focused on its core policy of continuing the political resistance against its main enemy in Tehran. After enduring years of pain and suffering in Iraq, the organization was able to successfully relocate to Albania in 2016. This astonishing resilience during the most agonizing and anguishing of periods in its history is a testament to the MEK's staying power, thanks to the dedication of its leadership and members, its treasure trove of experience, organizational dexterity, and mastery of strategy and tactics. Clearly, the organization could not have tolerated the monsoon of the regime's onslaught without enjoying popular backing among the Iranian people, enabling it to survive financially, logistically, spiritually, and psychologically.

Iran's future will be decided by the Iranian people alone. The world should respect the will of the Iranian people. There are some undeniable facts. The Iranian people want to overthrow the religious dictatorship. Iranian women demand respect for their basic rights, including the freedom to choose one's clothing. They have come to believe that these rights can only be realized by overthrowing the regime. All the evidence points to the fact that the separation of religion and state is a ubiquitous demand in Iran. The same atmosphere exists among Iran's ethnic and religious minorities, whose rights will only be realized in a democratic Iran.

The people of Iran rejected the monarchy in 1979. Torture and execution by the Shah's secret police, SAVAK, cannot simply be wiped off history books. In 1975, the Shah officially announced that Iran is a one-party system and anyone who disagrees with it must either leave Iran or land in prison. These are the undeniable realities of Iranian political history. There are no meaningful signs inside Iran that point to a popular desire for the rehabilitation of the former dictatorship. In fact, one of the slogans shouted in various universities and protests is the rejection of both the religious tyranny and the Shah's dictatorship.

Every Western government, and especially Washington, has a moral duty towards the Iranian people by avoiding any policy that directly or indirectly benefits the Iranian regime. These governments must stand with the Iranian people and their legitimate aspirations by adopting specific measures to benefit respect for human rights and internationally recognized standards.

As an example, silence and inaction in the face of the regime's terrorism abroad, including the plot to bomb the NCRI rally in Paris in June 2018, which was attended by hundreds of political dignitaries, including luminaries from the United States, is both immoral and an endangerment of our national security. Silence in the face of credible assassination threats against American officials and the regime's plots and preparations in this regard contradicts US national interests.

For this reason, in addition to the moral aspect, it is necessary for the US or any other country to have a correct grasp of Iranian society and its constituent elements, including the opposition forces, and to base their policies on concrete realities in Iran. Today's protests in Iran are rooted in a 43-year-old struggle. The West should align itself with the Iranian people and the organized opposition.

CPSIA information can be obtained
at www.ICGtesting.com
Printed in the USA
BVHW061733070123
655725BV00024B/1015